WIZ

ARMIES OF DEATH

The Kingdom of Allansia is under threat. Agglax the evil Zombie-Lord is amassing an army of undead warriors in eastern Allansia, beyond the Forest of Fiends. His army increases in size with every attack it makes on the local villages and every day its ranks are swelled with slaughtered victims under Agglax's evil spell. Unless they are stopped now, the undead will take over the entire kingdom.

YOU are Allansia's only hope. Your mission is to raise an army which will defeat the terrifying undead troops ... but how can YOU conquer an army which grows in numbers with every battle it fights?

Two dice, a pencil and an eraser are all YOU need to embark on this thrilling adventure, which is complete with its elaborate combat system and a score-sheet to record your gains and losses.

Many dangers lie ahead and success is by no means certain. It's up to YOU to decide which routes to follow, which dangers to risk and which adversaries to fight!

The Fighting Fantasy Gamebooks

1. The Warlock of Firetop Mountain
2. The Citadel of Chaos
3. Deathtrap Dungeon
4. Creature of Havoc
5. City of Thieves
6. Crypt of the Sorcerer
7. House of Hell
8. Forest of Doom
9. Sorcery! 1: The Shamutanti Hills
10. Caverns of the Snow Witch
11. Sorcery! 2: Kharé – Cityport of Traps
12. Trial of Champions
13. Sorcery! 3: The Seven Serpents
14. Armies of Death (September 2003)
15. Sorcery! 4: The Crown of Kings (September 2003)
16. Return to Firetop Mountain (December 2003)
17. Island of the Lizard King (December 2003)

IAN LIVINGSTONE

ARMIES OF DEATH

ILLUSTRATED BY NIK WILLIAMS

Wizard Books

This edition published in the UK in 2003 by Wizard Books,
an imprint of Icon Books Ltd., Grange Road, Duxford,
Cambridge CB2 4QF. Tel. 01763 208008. Fax. 01763 208080
e-mail: wizard@iconbooks.co.uk
www.iconbooks.co.uk/wizard

First published by the Penguin Group in 1988

Sold in the UK, Europe, South Africa and Asia by
Faber and Faber Ltd., 3 Queen Square, London WC1N 3AU
or their agents

Distributed in the UK, Europe, South Africa and Asia by
TBS Ltd., Frating Distribution Centre, Colchester Road,
Frating Green, Colchester C07 7DW

This edition published in Australia in 2003 by
Allen & Unwin Pty. Ltd., PO Box 8500, 83 Alexander Street,
Crows Nest, NSW 2065

Distributed in Canada by Penguin Books Canada,
10 Alcorn Avenue, Suite 300, Toronto, Ontario M4V 3B2

ISBN 1 84046 436 4

Text copyright © 1988 Ian Livingstone
Illustrations copyright © 1988 Nik Williams

The author and artist have asserted their moral rights.

No part of this book may be reproduced in any form, or by any
means, without prior permission in writing from the publisher.

Printed and bound in Australia by
McPherson's Printing Group, Victoria

*For Steve, Skye, Mark, Peter and Clive
of the Games Night Club*

CONTENTS

FIGHTING MONSTERS

9

ADVENTURE SHEET

18

BACKGROUND

20

ARMIES OF DEATH

23

FIGHTING MONSTERS

Before embarking on your adventure, you must first determine your own strengths and weaknesses.

Use dice to determine your initial SKILL, STAMINA and LUCK scores. On pages 18–19 there is an *Adventure Sheet* which you may use to record the details of an adventure. On it you will find boxes for recording your SKILL, STAMINA and LUCK scores.

You are advised to either record your scores on the *Adventure Sheet* in pencil, or make photocopies of the page to use in future adventures.

Skill, Stamina and Luck

Roll one die. Add 6 to this number and enter this total in the SKILL box on the *Adventure Sheet*.

Roll both dice. Add 12 to the number rolled and enter this total in the STAMINA box.

There is also a LUCK box. Roll one die, add 6 to this number and enter this total in the LUCK box.

For reasons that will be explained below, SKILL, STAMINA and LUCK scores change constantly during an adventure. You must keep an accurate record of these scores and for this reason you are advised either to write small in the boxes or to keep an eraser handy.

But never rub out your *Initial* scores. Although you may be awarded additional SKILL, STAMINA and LUCK points, these totals may never exceed your *Initial* scores except on very rare occasions, and you will be instructed when this is to happen.

Your SKILL score reflects your swordsmanship and general fighting expertise; the higher the better. Your STAMINA score reflects your general constitution, your will to survive, your determination and overall fitness; the higher your STAMINA score, the longer you will be able to survive. Your LUCK score indicates how naturally lucky a person you are. Luck – and magic – are facts of life in the fantasy kingdom you are about to explore.

Single Combat

You will often come across pages in the book which instruct you to fight a creature of some sort. You must resolve the battle as described below.

First record the creature's SKILL and STAMINA scores in the first vacant Enemy Encounter Box on your *Adventure Sheet*. The scores for each creature are given in the book each time you have an encounter. The sequence of combat is then:

1. Roll the two dice for the creature. Add its SKILL score. This total is the creature's *Attack Strength*.

2. Roll the two dice for yourself. Add your current SKILL. This total is your *Attack Strength*.

3. Whose *Attack Strength* is higher? If your *Attack Strength* is higher, you have wounded the creature. If the creature's *Attack Strength* is higher, it has wounded you. (If both are the same, you have both missed – start the next *Attack Round* from step 1 above.)

4. If you wounded the creature, subtract 2 points from its STAMINA score. You may use LUCK here to do additional damage (see 'Using Luck in Battles' below).

5. If the creature wounded you, subtract 2 points from your STAMINA score. You may use LUCK to minimize the damage (see below).

6. Make the appropriate changes to either the creature's or your own STAMINA scores (and your LUCK score if you used LUCK) and begin the next *Attack Round* (repeat steps 1–6).

7. This continues until the STAMINA score of either you or the creature you are fighting has been reduced to zero (death).

Battles

Unlike other Fighting Fantasy Gamebooks, you are not alone all the time on this adventure. You command an army of soldiers made up of units of various races. You start your expedition with Dwarfs, Elves, Warriors and Knights, and others will join your army during the course of the adventure. Soldiers killed in battles are always lost in blocks of five, and if more than one race is engaged in a battle, you may choose which ones are lost; for example, if you have employed Dwarfs and Knights against Goblins and receive 15 casualties, you may lose 15 Dwarfs; or 15 Knights; or 10 Dwarfs and 5 Knights; or 5 Dwarfs and 10 Knights. Remember always to make the necessary adjustments on your *Adventure Sheet*. Soldiers lost in ways other than in battle are deducted in the same way.

Fighting Skirmish Battles

SKIRMISH BATTLE RESULTS

SITUATION

		Superior	Even	Inferior
	1	5A	10A	15A
	2	5E	5A	10A
DIE	3	5E	5A	5A
ROLL	4	5E	5E	5A
	5	10E	5E	5E
	6	15E	10E	5E

A = *Allied troops*   E = *Enemy troops*

From time to time on your adventure, you will fight *Skirmish Battles*. To fight a *Skirmish Battle*, follow the combat sequence below.

1. Make a note of the number of your troops, not including yourself.

2. Make a note of the number of enemy troops.

3. Compare the size of the two armies and assess the situation. For example, if 10 of your Dwarfs were fighting 10 Hobgoblins, the situation would be *Even*. If 10 Dwarfs were up against 15 enemy Hobgoblins, your situation would be *Inferior*, whereas 15 of your Dwarfs against 10 Hobgoblins would be *Superior*.

4. Roll one die and see what figure is given in the *Skirmish Battle Results* Table (opposite) for the appropriate *Situation* column.

5. Deduct the number of troops lost from either the enemy army or your own.

6. If troops remain alive on both sides, return to step 1 or 2, adjusting the number of troops for the side that has just incurred losses.

7. If your own troops are wiped out, you too will have perished in battle.

Fighting More Than One Creature

If you come across more than one creature in a particular encounter, the instructions on that page will tell you how to handle the battle. Sometimes you will treat them as a single opponent; sometimes you will fight each one in turn.

Luck

At various times during your adventure, either in battles or when you come across situations in which you could either be lucky or unlucky (details of these are given on the pages themselves), you may call on your LUCK to make the outcome more favourable. But beware! Using LUCK is a risky business, and if you are *un*lucky, the results could be disastrous.

The procedure for using your LUCK is as follows: roll two dice. If the number rolled is equal to or less than your current LUCK score, you have been lucky and the result will go in your favour. If the number rolled is higher than your current LUCK score, you have been unlucky and you will be penalized.

This procedure is known as *Testing your Luck*. Each time you *Test your Luck*, you must subtract 1 point from your current LUCK score. Thus you will soon realize that the more you rely on your LUCK, the more risky this will become.

Using Luck in Battles

On certain pages of the book you will be told to *Test your Luck* and will be told the consequences of your being lucky or unlucky. However, in battles, you always have the option of using your LUCK either to inflict a more serious wound on a creature you have just wounded, or to minimize the effects of a wound the creature has just inflicted on you.

If you have just wounded the creature, you may *Test your Luck* as described above. If you are Lucky, you have inflicted a severe wound and may subtract an extra 2 points from the creature's STAMINA score. However, if you are Unlucky, the wound was a mere graze and you must restore 1 point to the creature's STAMINA (i.e. instead of scoring the normal 2 points of damage, you have now scored only 1).

If the creature has just wounded you, you may *Test your Luck* to try to minimize the wound. If you are Lucky, you have managed to avoid the full damage of the blow. Restore 1 point of STAMINA (i.e. instead of doing 2 points of damage it has done only 1). If you are Unlucky, you have taken a more serious blow. Subtract 1 extra STAMINA point.

Remember that you must subtract 1 point from your LUCK score every time you *Test your Luck*.

Restoring Skill, Stamina and Luck

Skill

Your SKILL score will not change much during your adventure. Occasionally, a page may give instructions to increase or decrease your SKILL score. A Magic Weapon may increase your SKILL, but remember that only one weapon can be used at a time! You cannot claim 2 SKILL bonuses for carrying two Magic Swords. Your SKILL score can never exceed its *Initial* value unless specifically instructed.

Stamina

Your STAMINA score will change a lot during your adventure as you fight monsters and undertake arduous tasks. As you near your goal, your STAMINA level may be dangerously low and battles may be particularly risky, so be careful!

Unlike some Fighting Fantasy Gamebooks, you do not start your adventure with Provisions. However, during the course of the adventure, there will be opportunities for you to regain STAMINA points in various ways.

Remember also that your STAMINA score may never exceed its *Initial* value unless specifically instructed on a page.

Luck

Additions to your LUCK score are awarded through the adventure when you have been particularly lucky. Details are given on the pages of this book. Remember that, as with SKILL and STAMINA, your LUCK score may never exceed its *Initial* value unless specifically instructed on a page.

Alternative Dice

If you do not have a pair of dice handy, dice rolls are printed throughout the book at the bottom of the pages. Flicking rapidly through the book and stopping on a page will give you a random dice roll. If you need to 'roll' only one die, read only the first printed die; if two, total the two dice symbols.

ADVENTURE SHEET

SKILL	STAMINA	LUCK
Initial Skill =	*Initial Stamina* =	*Initial Luck* =

SOLDIERS

WARRIORS
100

DWARFS
50

ELVES
50

KNIGHTS
20

OTHERS

GOLD PIECES
700

TREASURE

ENEMY ENCOUNTER BOXES

Skill = *Stamina* =	*Skill* = *Stamina* =	*Skill* = *Stamina* =
Skill = *Stamina* =	*Skill* = *Stamina* =	*Skill* = *Stamina* =
Skill = *Stamina* =	*Skill* = *Stamina* =	*Skill* = *Stamina* =
Skill = *Stamina* =	*Skill* = *Stamina* =	*Skill* = *Stamina* =

BACKGROUND

Fame and fortune are two things which most adventurers crave and, having survived Baron Sukumvit's infamous Deathtrap Dungeon, you now have both. It was thought impossible for anybody to battle their way successfully through the deadly dungeon in Fang, which was protected by the baron's cunning Trialmasters. Yet somehow you survived and claimed the purse of 20,000 Gold Pieces in the Trial of Champions.

Now, wherever you walk in Fang, you are cheered, and in the taverns where you drink, people ask you about your perilous journey through the dungeon. 'Was there a Bone Devil in the dungeon?' . . . 'Did you see the beautiful Siren?' . . . 'How did you overcome the Liche Queen?' . . . 'What does a Coldclaw look like?' . . . 'What is the colour of Mutant Orc's blood?' Everybody is in awe of you and wants to know all about the evil dungeon. But the constant attention soon becomes tiring and you resolve to set off on another quest as soon as possible. Besides, there is a new threat to Allansia which is gathering strength in the east. Before you set off, you decide to spend some of your hard-earned prize money. You commission a small castle to be built for you on the south bank of the River Kok while you are away; with the remaining 6,000 Gold Pieces, you decide to hire soldiers to make an army! Recently there have been sightings of a large number of Orcs and Goblins in the Forest of Fiends. There is a rumour that their leader is Agglax the Shadow Demon.

A Shadow Demon, as everybody knows, is a servant of the Demon Princes and a commander of the Legions of the Damned. Since their banishment to the Void after the First Battle of Titan, however, the Demon Princes were thought to have been defeated for ever. And yet one of their servants is now reported to have been seen. This tale comes from an old scavenger calling himself Drek who discovered a ruined temple near Zengis. Scratching around in the dirt in search of anything he might be able to sell, Drek found a black clay pot, corked and sealed with black wax. His curiosity proved too much for him and he broke the pot on a stone, hoping that it might contain gold or jewels. But his excitement soon turned to terror at the sight of what happened next. As soon as the black pot broke apart, Drek was deafened by the most hideous and evil cry that he had ever heard in his life. Slowly a mist started to form, growing ever larger and darker, until it coalesced in the shape of a black robe wrapped around a body that was invisible save only for two pulsating, blood-red eyes. Drek screamed in total fear, but the Shadow Demon he had released simply turned and disappeared. The chaos-spawn was to grow again on Titan.

On the strength of Drek's story, you post recruitment notices all over Fang. The honour of fighting alongside someone of your renown – with the added bonus of payment in gold – draws a long line of hopeful warriors outside the tavern where you intend to hire your soldiers. Many are alone, others come in groups, but all are eager to sign up. Some tell of old adventures, others of monsters slain. But you recognize the qualities you seek and before nightfall your troops are chosen. Not knowing what dangers you will face, you decide not to hire all the warriors who have come, so as to have some gold left for the journey. You count the commission sheets and find that you have hired 100 Warriors, 50 Dwarfs, 50 Elven Archers and 20 Knights. In the morning you buy food, provisions and baggage mules. When everything is paid for, you are left with 700 Gold Pieces which you put in a wooden chest and strap to one of the mules. You make your way to the town square where your small army is assembled. Each unit leader is handed a yellow banner with the symbol of a burning sword emblazoned across it. To the cheers of the citizens of Fang, you lead your army out through the east gate towards an unknown and deadly foe.

NOW TURN TO 1.

1

You have marched no more than two hundred yards when a fat, bearded man, huffing and puffing, runs up alongside you. He is dressed as a sea captain, although his uniform is dirty and crumpled, and his grubby hat is dented. 'Begging your pardon,' gasps the captain, 'but would you listen to my offer? I have just docked my ship in Fang and found everybody full of excitement. It seems that you are the cause of it. They tell me that you are travelling east to fight some demon or something. Well, I don't know about any demons, but I'm willing to take you and your men on my ship as far as Zengis – for a small consideration, of course. Just think of all those miles you won't have to walk. Sail up the River Kok in Captain Barnock's good ship *Flying Toucan*. And only 50 Gold Pieces am I asking for this luxury passage. Now, that's a bargain, is it not?' says the old sea-dog. If you wish to sail on the *Flying Toucan*, turn to **37**. If you would rather continue marching, turn to **225**.

2

With your shield held above your head, you start to climb. The Blog shuffles between the upper branches, trying to get a clear shot at you. With only one hand free with which to climb, you suddenly lose your grip on a branch. *Test your Luck.* If you are Lucky, turn to **396**. If you are Unlucky, turn to **140**.

3

'I'm not interested in talking,' the rogue says sternly. 'Now shut up and go away.' If you decide to do as he says and move to another table where the three vagabonds are sitting, turn to **18**. If you would rather continue talking, turn to **152**.

4

Each Elf fires two arrows at the fifty Fire Imps. To determine how many Fire Imps are shot out of the sky, multiply the number of Elves in your army by two, then deduct the total of two dice, rolled for the number of misses. Against the remaining Fire Imps, you must fight a *Skirmish Battle* with thirty Warriors. If you win, turn to **316**.

5

The backpack hits its target, sending the sword crashing to the floor with a loud clatter. The Elf starts to cry with relief as you cut the ropes that are binding her. 'Thank you,' she sobs, 'thank you for saving my life.' She then pulls a ring off her finger and says, 'Please take this ring as a token of my gratitude. It will bring you luck.' If you wish to take the ring, turn to **270**. If you prefer to refuse her gift, retrieve your backpack and rejoin your men outside, turn to **211**.

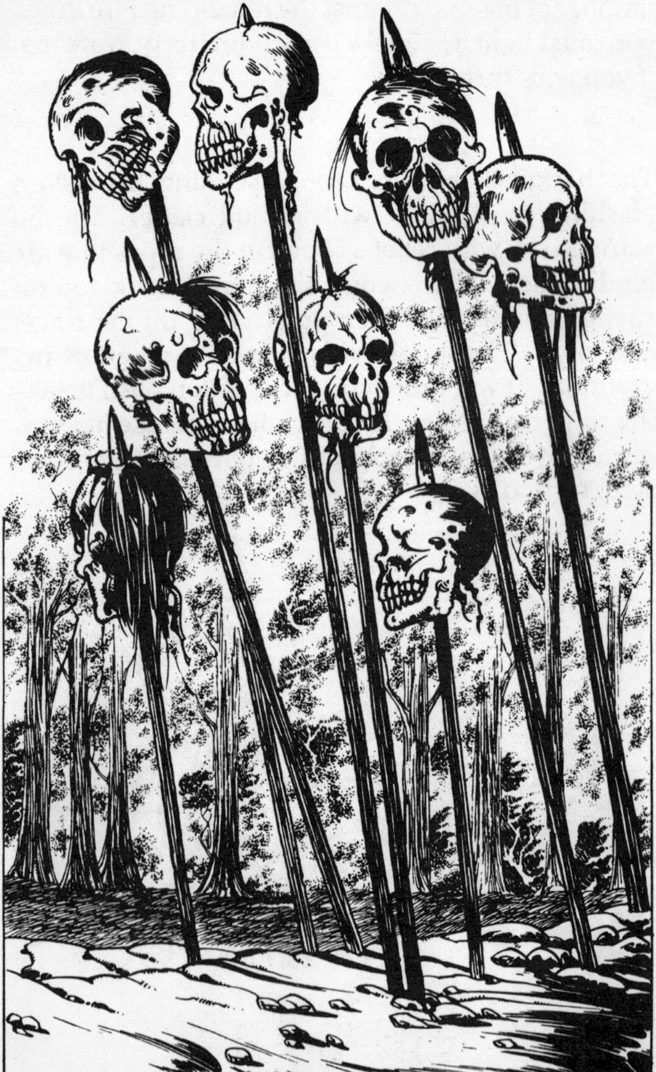

6

Your army marches two abreast along the path and makes good progress. The path ends at another clearing. Here you see many spears stuck in the ground, their tips pointing upwards, on which human skulls are skewered. If you wish to walk through the clearing, turn to **48**. If you would rather walk around it under cover of the trees, turn to **389**.

7

Your losses are greater than you had expected. Ten Warriors and ten Elves died on board the *Flying Toucan*, and five Dwarfs and fifteen Knights were drowned in the river, dragged under the water by the weight of their armour. Lose 1 point from your LUCK. The survivors seem reassured to have firm ground underfoot once more and are keen to start marching. You decide to set off straight away, hoping to reach Zengis the following day. Turn to **366**.

8

'Well answered, my friend,' says the Oracle. 'Now, the final test. I want you to perform some magic for me. You can hear me, but you cannot see me. I think we should be equals. Make yourself invisible!' If you own a pet Hopper, turn to **224**. If you do not own this creature, turn to **108**.

9

The arrows all miss the fast-climbing target, and soon the Wyvern and its rider are no more than a speck in the sky heading towards the eastern horizon. Aware that Agglax might send more would-be assassins, you give the order to march on to Claw, but with your troops in much closer formation. Turn to **220**.

10

You reach into your backpack and pull out the brass owl. 'Put it down on the floor,' continues the Oracle. 'Good. But, alas, I am very greedy and want something else. Do you have a green vase you could give me?' If you have a green vase and can remember how many Gold Pieces it cost, turn to that number. If you do not possess a green vase, turn to **297**.

11

You feel no different for having drunk the water, apart from feeling more refreshed. Neither poisoned nor filled with sudden energy, you walk rather disappointedly through the cave and down the passage in the wall opposite. Turn to **221**.

12

Not long after midnight, something disturbs your sleep and you wake to see a bright moonlit sky. Barely moving your head, you look left and right and see a shadow moving near some barrels tied amidships. On the bridge there is no sign of the lookout and you immediately sense danger. Grabbing your sword, you tip-toe towards the barrels, crouched down. Something that glints in the moonlight is suddenly hurled at you without warning. Instinctively you duck. Roll two dice. If the number rolled is the same as or less than your SKILL, turn to **246**. If the number rolled is greater than your SKILL, turn to **267**.

13

There is a loud sound of clashing steel as the two armies meet. The fighting is fierce and bloody and, although heavily outnumbered, you gain a little ground. In the centre of the fighting, you find yourself battling it out with one of the largest Trolls of all, the fearsome Hill Troll.

HILL TROLL   SKILL 9   STAMINA 10

If you win, turn to **142**.

14

You find yourself the only challenger, everybody else being unwilling to take on the great Big Belly Man. The Dwarf tells you that there is a purse of 100 Gold Pieces for the person who can defeat Big Belly Man and that the entry fee is 10 Gold Pieces. You pay him the money and sit down at the table to await the return of the champion. Yet another cheer goes up as the crowd parts to let the big man back to the table. Two more Dwarfs follow him, each wearing cook's clothes and carrying a tray with an enormous steaming pie on top. Big Belly Man sits at the table and shuffles his chair forward to squeeze his stomach into the recess. A pie is then put in front of you and your nostrils twitch at the mingled aroma of fish and custard. You are handed a wooden spoon and the Dwarf then shouts, 'Ready! Steady! Go!' You plunge your spoon into the pie and begin to eat.

To determine who wins, dice must be rolled. Roll one die and add this number to your SKILL score. After making a note of the total, roll the die again and add the new number to Big Belly Man's pie-eating ability, which is 13. Note this total too. Roll the die again and add the number to your current score, and then again for Big Belly Man. Continue until Big Belly Man's score reaches 40 first (turn to **388**) or your own score reaches 40 first (turn to **60**).

15

Through a gap in the bushes, you notice the entrance to a small cave not far from the path. If you wish to look inside the cave, turn to **87**. If you would rather march on, turn to **181**.

16

The guard also manages to dispose of his attacker and thanks you for raising the alarm. You tell him in future to keep his eyes open on both the land and the river. The other guards report nothing strange, so you return to your blanket and sleep. You set off on your march again in the early morning, hoping to reach Zengis by nightfall. After an hour or so, you meet an old man walking in the opposite direction. 'You're the one who's going to fight Agglax, aren't you?' he says boldly. You nod in agreement. 'Good!' he continues. 'Then I suggest that when you come to the fork in the river, you follow the north branch until you reach the village of Claw. There are plenty of Hill Men up there who would be ready to join your army.' You thank the old man for the information and press on eastwards. After an hour you come to the fork in the river that the old man was talking about. If you wish to follow the north branch, turn to **350**. If you would rather cross over the new branch and follow the main river eastwards, turn to **49**.

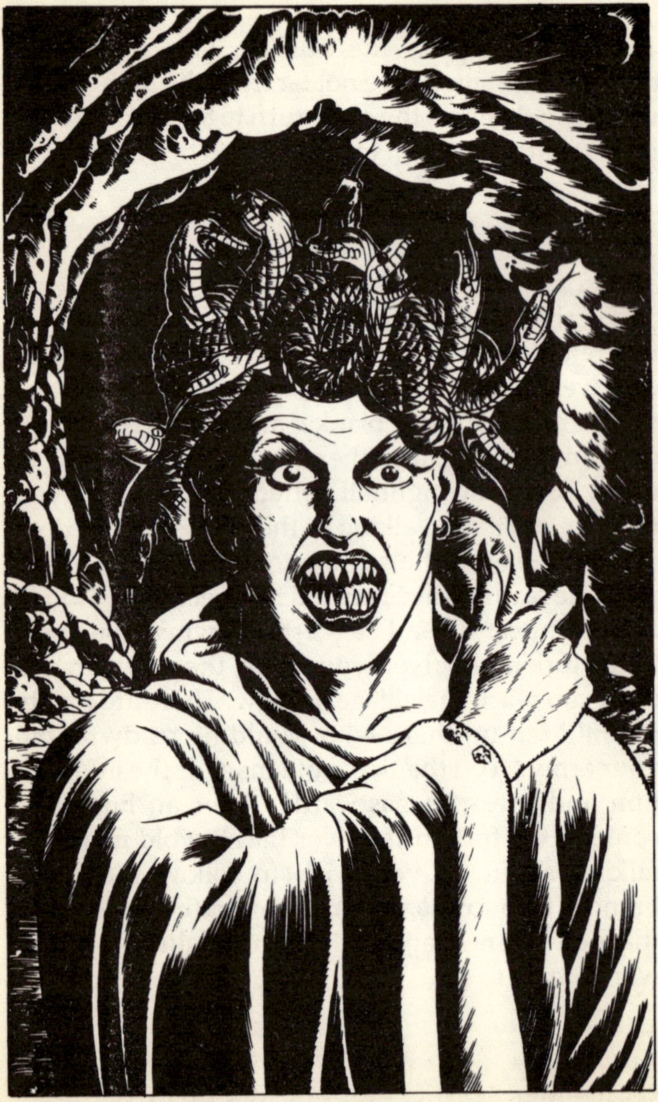

17

You round a corner of the passageway and see the silhouette of something blocking your way. It appears to be a human shape and a robe covers its head. As you move closer to see better, the figure suddenly turns back the robe to reveal a woman's hideous face with a mass of wriggling snakes on her head in place of hair. Looking into her sickly red eyes, you are caught by the Medusa's stare. Your limbs immediately stiffen and moments later you are nothing but solid stone.

18

You sit down at the table with the three vagabonds and they immediately introduce themselves as Enk, Laz and Jip. They ask you what you are doing in Zengis. If you wish to tell them about your mission, turn to **395**. If you would rather tell them that you are in Zengis to visit your cousin, turn to **35**.

19

The girl smiles as she hands you your winnings and says, 'What about a tip for a hard-working girl?' If you wish to toss her a Gold Piece, turn to **347**. If you would rather leave the gambling-hall at once, turn to **212**.

20

'Excellent!' booms the Oracle's voice as you pull out the vase from your backpack. 'Now I'm going to ask you a question, but I'll let fate decide on its difficulty. Let me roll my dice.' *Test your Luck*. If you are Lucky, turn to **341**. If you are Unlucky, turn to **263**.

21

Before the River Raiders close with your ship, another fireball is flung from the catapult. *Test your Luck*. If you are Lucky, turn to **159**. If you are Unlucky, turn to **74**.

22

As you enter the stable, the Shapechanger throws the half-strangled Dwarf to the floor and turns its bloodied claws towards you.

SHAPECHANGER SKILL 10 STAMINA 10

If you win, turn to 361.

23

At such a short range, the hurled rock is deadly. It crashes into the side of your head and you fall down among the other brave soldiers who died to save Allansia. Demoralized by your death, your army turns and flees. Agglax is victorious.

24

The Goblin topples out of its saddle and crashes to the ground, dying with the impact. A search of the Goblin's pockets reveals a bowstring and five arrowheads, which are of no use to you, but you also discover a bone pendant with the number '8' scratched on the base. Keep the pendant if you wish, before giving the order to march on to Claw. Turn to 220.

25

You hold on to the rope and let an Elf lower himself down into the dark hole, holding a burning torch between his teeth. You watch him drop on to the floor of a large chamber. 'Nothing in here,' comes a cry from below, 'except for a terrible stink of animal droppings. There's a tunnel leading away from the cavern, but I can't see where it leads to. Do you want me to go down it?' If you wish the Elf to go down the tunnel, turn to **198**. If you tell him to climb back up the rope so that you can leave the clearing, turn to **315**.

26

You decide to spare the life of the barman and let him stagger across to his friends to have his wounds attended to. Then you turn to the crowd and say, 'I am here in search of brave warriors to join my army to fight the Shadow Demon that brings death to

Allansia. My payment is 10 Gold Pieces, but I want only the best fighters.' Within half an hour you have fifteen Warriors signed up; you tell them where to go to join your waiting army; they are to meet Lexon, who will pay them (deduct 150 Pieces from your *Adventure Sheet*). Seeing no other characters of interest, you leave 'The Black Dragon' to see what else you can find in Zengis. Turn to **382**.

27

'Well, if you don't want to visit the Oracle, there's not much point in going to the Starstone Caves. Is there anywhere else you would like to get to?' You reply that you would like to go through the Forest of Fiends. Turn to **319**.

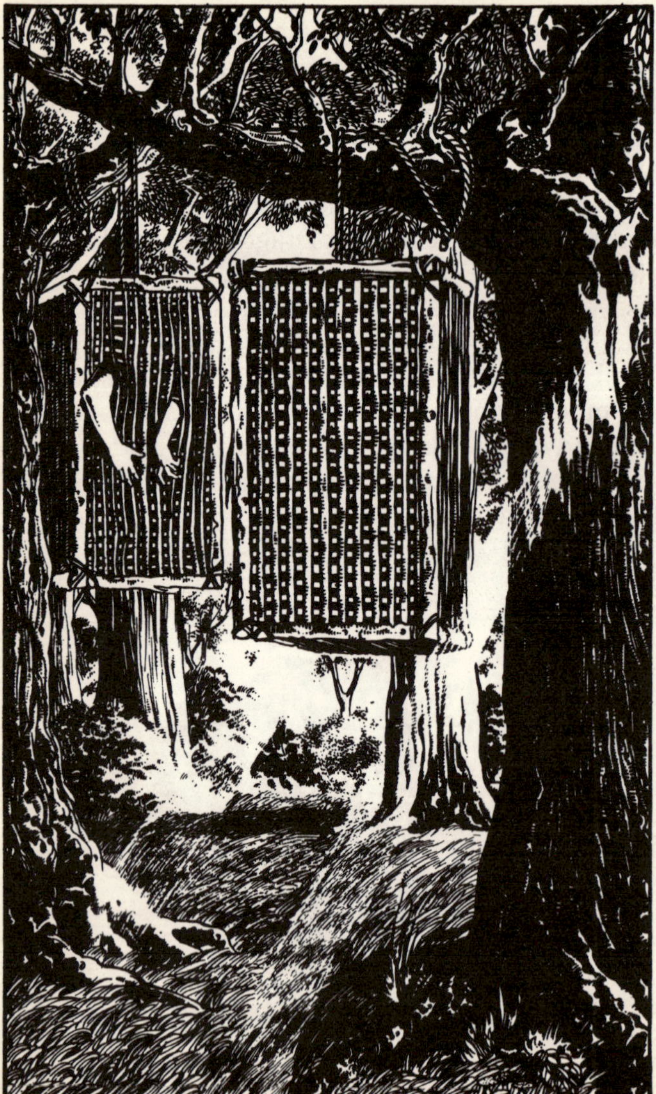

28

Ten of the Elves accompany you as you walk stealthily into the wood, sword in hand. You can hear the cries for help quite clearly yourself now, as you slip quickly from behind one tree to the next. Suddenly, in front of you you see a wooden cage suspended by a rope from the branch of a tree. You see another close by with two arms sticking out between the wooden boards. You count eleven cages in total, each one probably holding a man. If you wish to make yourself known to the men in the cages, turn to **182**. If you would rather retreat quietly out of the wood and rejoin your troops, turn to **143**.

29

You avenge the death of your troops with one quick thrust of your sword. You call out to your Warriors to return to the path and march on. Turn to **130**.

30

You pay the leader of the Northmen 100 Gold Pieces and give the order for him and his men to climb on board ship. As you set sail once more, the leader walks over to you; despite his stare from piercing ice-blue eyes, you feel you can trust him. 'My name is Laas,' he says with a warm smile. 'Would you allow me to bestow a gift upon you?' If you want to take the gift, turn to **358**. If you would rather refuse politely, turn to **390**.

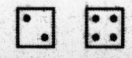

31

You climb down a metal-runged ladder that is secured to the side of the wall, until you reach the sewer below. The foul stench rising from the sludge that is flowing slowly by makes you heave. Looking down the sewer you see what appears to be the flickering flame of a candle and you can just hear the sound of a whispering voice. You are convinced that there must be more Sewer Goblins ahead. If you wish to walk down the sewer, turn to **232**. If you would rather climb back up the ladder, turn to **300**.

32

'You are very unobservant, my friend,' the Oracle informs you solemnly. 'I am unable to assist anybody who is not worthy of my powers. Goodbye.' The eyes of the stone face close again and you are left to ponder what to do next. You hear a grating sound behind you; looking round, you see a section of wall sliding back. You have no alternative but to step into the tunnel that has appeared. Turn to **280**.

33

Many men struggle through the marsh to help you, attacking the Mudgrinder from all sides. But its tough hide is hard to pierce and it is all you can do to defend yourself. You realize that you will have to attack its soft underbelly so you lunge forward with your sword as the Mudgrinder rears up to attack some Dwarfs to its left. Roll two dice. If the total is the same or less than your SKILL, turn to **392**. If the total is greater than your SKILL, turn to **256**.

34

Twenty warriors cross safely before you step on to the bridge yourself. You are about halfway across when suddenly a rope snaps, sending everybody on the bridge plummeting to their deaths at the bottom of the chasm.

35

'That's strange,' says Enk. 'A lot of people seem to come to Zengis to visit relatives. Nobody ever seems to be here on business – not that we don't believe you, or anything like that. Where does your cousin live? Perhaps we can give you directions?' Will you reply:

Rubble Street?	Turn to 92
That it is none of their business?	Turn to 223
That you must be on your way?	Turn to 311

36

'Come on, follow me,' Thog says jovially to hearten the nervous troops. 'There's nothing more than a few trees and a couple of monkeys.' As you venture into the forest, the daylight quickly fades under a thick canopy of leaves overhead, and the whole place is deathly quiet. 'The creatures are watching us,' whispers Thog, 'but the little ones around the edge won't do us any harm. It's later on that we should start to get worried. We'll go right here to avoid the Tree Men.' Your army threads its way through the forest, and on into its darkest depths. Turn to **180**.

37

Following Captain Barnock, you lead your men down to the docks where the *Flying Toucan* is moored. It is an old ship and, like the captain, is in very poor condition. But this hardly comes as a surprise to you, as nothing of much worth ever comes out of Port Blacksand. You tell your men to go aboard and pay Captain Barnock his 50 Gold Pieces (deduct these from your *Adventure Sheet*). The captain shouts the order to set sail, and you watch the motley crew from the bridge as they haul on the ropes, climb the rigging and unfurl the sails. Within twenty minutes, Fang has faded from view as your river journey gets under way. Everybody is in high spirits and even the Dwarfs and Elves forget their differences and chat together, united in their desire to rid Allansia of the Shadow Demon. At the bow you see a group of Warriors leaning over the side of the ship, staring at the river. Suddenly one of them points upriver and shouts, 'Look! A barrel, floating towards us.' You look over the side and see the large, sealed barrel bobbing in the water. If you want to order one of your men to dive into the water in order to haul in the barrel, turn to **145**. If you would rather sail on without stopping, turn to **346**.

38

You come across a worn track which runs north and south. You decide to follow it to the south and soon you arrive at a signpost which also points south and reads, 'Karn – 5 miles'. If you wish to keep heading south towards Karn, turn to **266**. If you would rather head south-east, turn to **331**.

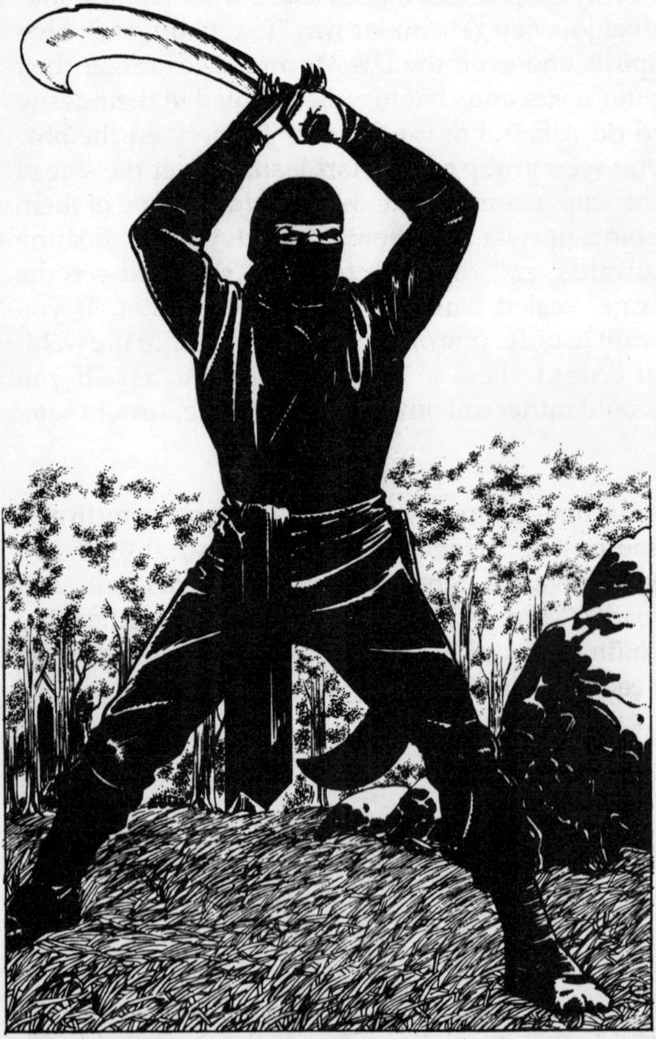

39

Agglax shrinks back in his chair when he sees the Crystal of Light in your hands. Covering his face with his hands, he suddenly jumps down from the chair and runs away, hissing orders at a group of his black-robed Elite Fanatics standing close by. One blocks your way to Agglax; his curved sword held in both hands above his head, the grim assassin is more than willing to die to save his master. 'Tanaka San say you die!' he shrieks as he darts forward to cut you down where you stand.

ELITE FANATIC   SKILL 10   STAMINA 10

If you win, turn to 254.

40

You tell the barman that you have no time or inclination to make a fool of yourself by performing drunken tricks for his seedy customers, and that you are here to hire brave warriors to fight Agglax, the Shadow Demon. A frown pushes down his dark, bushy eyebrows as he suddenly looks intensely interested in what you are saying. 'Well, why didn't you tell me that in the first place?' he says with a smile which suddenly lights up his face. 'I know all the best fighters in town and most of them are in here now!' Within half an hour you have another fifteen Warriors signed up; you tell them where to go to join your waiting army; they are to meet Lexon, who will pay them 10 Gold Pieces each (deduct 150 Gold Pieces from your *Adventure Sheet*). You finally shake hands with the big barman and leave 'The Black Dragon' to find other things or people of interest in Zengis. Turn to **382**.

41

You stand in the centre of the floor, sword in hand, to face the warrior woman. Without warning she suddenly leaps forward, cutting her sword down through the air. Instinctively you raise your sword to ward off the blow.

MAX   SKILL 11   STAMINA 7

If you are the first to strike, turn to **195**. If Max strikes the first blow, turn to **385**.

42

Drinking the Water of the Gods has saved you from a horrible death. The radiating glow gradually dies down and soon you are back to normal. You look round the cave and find no exits leading from it. A man's face is carved in the rock wall, its eyes closed and its mouth open. As you walk over to examine it closer, the eyes open and a deep voice booms out of the mouth, saying, 'I am the Oracle. Although you are not welcome here, I admire your determination and effort. No matter how noble your cause, you must pay for the answers to your questions. I too will ask you questions in return. Answer any incorrectly and you will pay with your life. I will start the proceedings, as I know everything. First, you may start by bestowing gifts upon me. You were in Zengis recently. I hope you took the trouble to buy me a brass owl, and I must know how much you paid for it.' If you have a brass owl and can remember how many Gold Pieces you paid for it, turn to that number. If you do not have a brass owl, turn to **206**.

43

By now many of your men are awake; none of them appears to have come to any harm, apart from the lookout who is nursing a sore head, having been attacked from behind by the midnight raider. An extra man is put on watch while everybody else settles down to sleep once again. Not long after dawn, Captain Barnock gives the order to set sail upriver. Turn to **188**.

44

'Your luck is in, my friend,' continues the Oracle. 'But I am greedy and desire something else. Now, do you have a green vase?' If you have a green vase and can remember how many Gold Pieces it cost, turn to that number. If you do not possess a green vase, turn to **297**.

45

The ring fits perfectly on the finger and you watch with amazement as the clenched fist slowly opens. Sparkling in the middle of the stone palm lies a beautiful crystal. The king's lips suddenly open and a voice booms out, 'I give you the Crystal of Light!' You take the crystal and run back to your waiting troops, full of excitement. After showing them your treasure, you march on along the path. Turn to **130**.

46

The key turns in the slot and you hear a faint click. You then hear a hissing sound and inhale some of the gas that is escaping from the slot before you have a chance to realize what is happening. It is a deadly poison and you slump to the ground, clutching your throat and gasping for air. Your quest is over.

47

'I'm sure you'll find this crow very good company. His name is Billy and he even understands the odd word in Orcish. Ten Gold Pieces is an absolute bargain for such a fine crow, if I say so myself.' If you wish to buy the crow, turn to **245**. If you would rather leave the shop without buying the crow, turn to **218**.

48

A shiver runs down your spine as you walk between the spears. In the middle of the clearing you find a mound of freshly turned-over earth and a shovel lying near by. If you wish to dig into the mound, turn to **98**. If you would rather keep walking, turn to **315**.

49

The rest of the day passes without incident and, as the light begins to fade, you give the order to set up camp at a defensible spot no more than ten miles distant from Zengis. As you settle down to sleep, having feasted on stewed rabbit, your mind drifts over the events of the day, but within seconds you are asleep. If you are wearing a beetle amulet round your neck, turn to **128**. If you are not wearing this amulet, turn to **279**.

50

Early next morning you rouse your men and are soon marching south-east. At noon you stop for food but are soon on the march again. By late afternoon you can see a row of hills in the distance. 'Starstone Caves,' says a man from Zengis. You arrive at the caves before dusk and decide to enter them alone. With a candle in one hand and your sword in the other, you clamber down into the mouth of a large, dark cave. Turn to **219**.

51

Nobody has any belladonna. An hour later you are shaking uncontrollably in the grip of a raging fever. Hair begins to sprout from your cheeks and arms and your face begins to change shape until it resembles the Werewolf that bit you. Watching in horror, your troops make the anguished decision to put you out of your misery. Their leader dead and morale gone, your army abandons the crusade against Agglax.

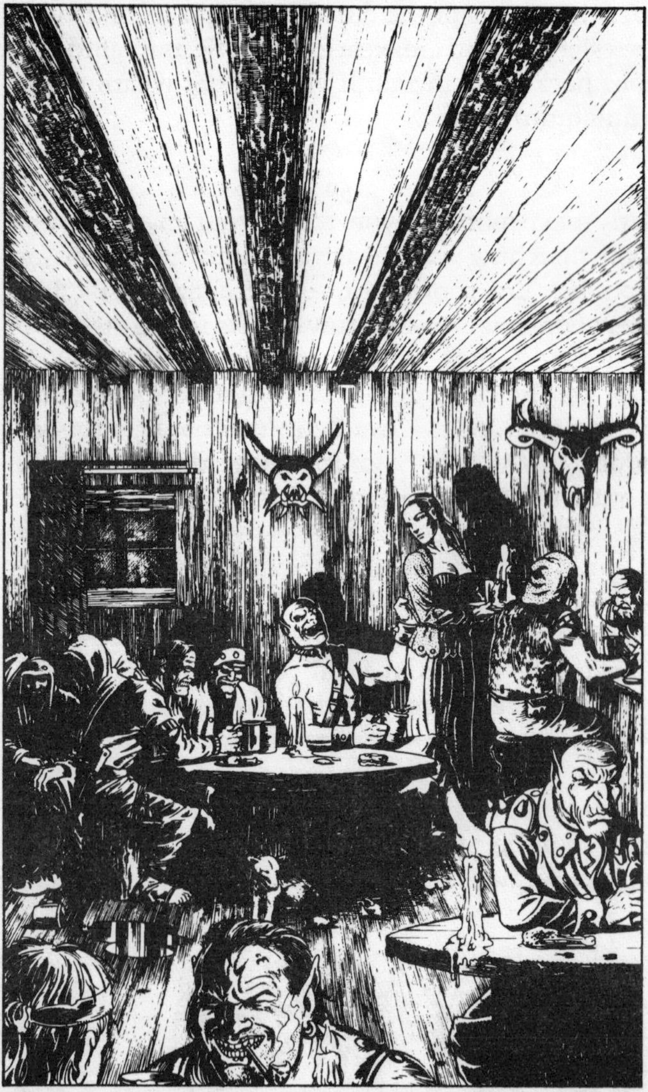

52

Two minutes later, you see a crooked wooden sign hanging over the door of an old wooden building. A crude drawing of a dragon is painted on it, above the words 'The Black Dragon'. There is much shouting and laughter coming from inside the tavern and you decide to enter at once. You climb a few well-worn stone steps and push open the heavy oak door. Even though it is daytime, the tavern is dark inside and candles are burning as the small grubby windows let in virtually no daylight. From the doorway you see that the tavern is bustling with life, although none of it looks too savoury. Groups of cloaked vagabonds are huddled together in dark corners, while boisterous rogues, much the worse for the ale they have already drunk, sit in the middle of the tavern insulting all who pass by them, including the harassed barmaids who have to squeeze between the tables carrying their loaded trays. You look from table to table and decide where to sit. Will you:

Sit at the bar?	Turn to **197**
Sit with a drunken rogue?	Turn to **378**
Sit with three vagabonds?	Turn to **18**

53

You soon come to a dead end and, sensing danger, turn and run. But before you can reach the mouth entrance, the upper stone teeth slide down to block your exit. Trapped inside the tunnel, death by starvation awaits you.

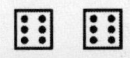

54

Half an hour after eating the apples, some of the soldiers become ill, yourself included. Deduct 2 points from your STAMINA and 1 point from your SKILL. Their health quickly deteriorates, and two die quite quickly. Before the day is over, five in all have died. Make the deduction on your *Adventure Sheet* and also deduct 1 point from your LUCK. You regret your decision to give the apples to your men and resolve not to be distracted from your main objective in future. Turn to **209**.

55

The servant of Agglax lies still on the ground, your sword having penetrated the only soft spot on its body, a small section of its otherwise rock-like stomach. Satisfied that the Rock Man will not fight on the side of Evil again, you give the order to march on. Turn to **114**.

56

Not knowing whether you have made the right decision to trust the vagabond, you nevertheless hand over 100 Gold Pieces to them. Laz takes out a map from under his robes and lays it out open on the table. Zengis is shown in the middle, and to the south is marked the village of Karn. Further south-east are the Starstone Caves. To the east of Zengis there is the Forest of Fiends, which starts where the River Kok splits and runs east, almost to the edge of the map. Laz takes out a black crayon and marks a large cross on the eastern edge of the map, just where the Forest of Fiends ends. 'That's where you'll find him,' says Laz. You fold up the map and put it in your tunic pocket. 'And your only hope of defeating Agglax rests on your visiting the Oracle,' whispers Jip. 'But whether or not the Oracle will talk to you is another matter. It depends on what mood the Oracle is in and what gifts you bring him. The Starstone Caves is where you'll find him.' You thank the vagabonds for the information and leave the tavern to explore Zengis further, wondering who the Oracle is. Turn to 382.

57
'So, you are another foolish person who wishes to see the Oracle, are you?' If you decide to reply 'Yes', turn to 144. If you prefer to reply 'No', turn to 27.

58
You suddenly catch sight of a grubby sackcloth bag lying hidden in the grass. You cut it open with your sword and, much to your surprise and pleasure, find 10 Gold Pieces. You call cheerfully to your men, telling them it is time to move on, and in minutes you are on the march again. Turn to 274.

59

Their numbers dwindling by the minute, your troops are completely demoralized. Only yards away from the enemy line, they turn and flee in disarray. You scream at them to stand and fight, but you cannot prevent them running away. Then many hands grab you and you are led in chains to Agglax for execution.

60

The crowd is stunned into silence when you drop your spoon into the empty bowl to signal victory. Big Belly Man, his mouth still crammed full of pie, shows his anger by brushing the pie bowl off the table so that it smashes on the floor. Shaking his head in disblief, the Dwarf hands you the purse containing 100 Gold Pieces. If you would like to stand on the table and make a speech about Agglax and your wish to hire ten stout fighters in exchange for the gold you have just won, turn to **165**. If you would rather leave with the gold, turn to **95**.

61

You shake your head and just manage to keep your balance as you hear the bellowing laugh of the barman behind you. You slump down in a chair at the table nearest to you, somewhat the worse for drink. Deduct 1 point from your STAMINA. Roll one die. If you roll 1–3, you find yourself sitting with a drunken rogue (turn to 378). If you roll 4–6, you find yourself sitting with three vagabonds (turn to 18).

62

Another Goblin sees you move towards the embattled Warrior. Recognizing you as the leader, the Goblin points its crossbow at you, takes careful aim and fires. If you hired Max's Marauders in Zengis, turn to 153. If you did not hire the warrior woman's fighters, turn to 339.

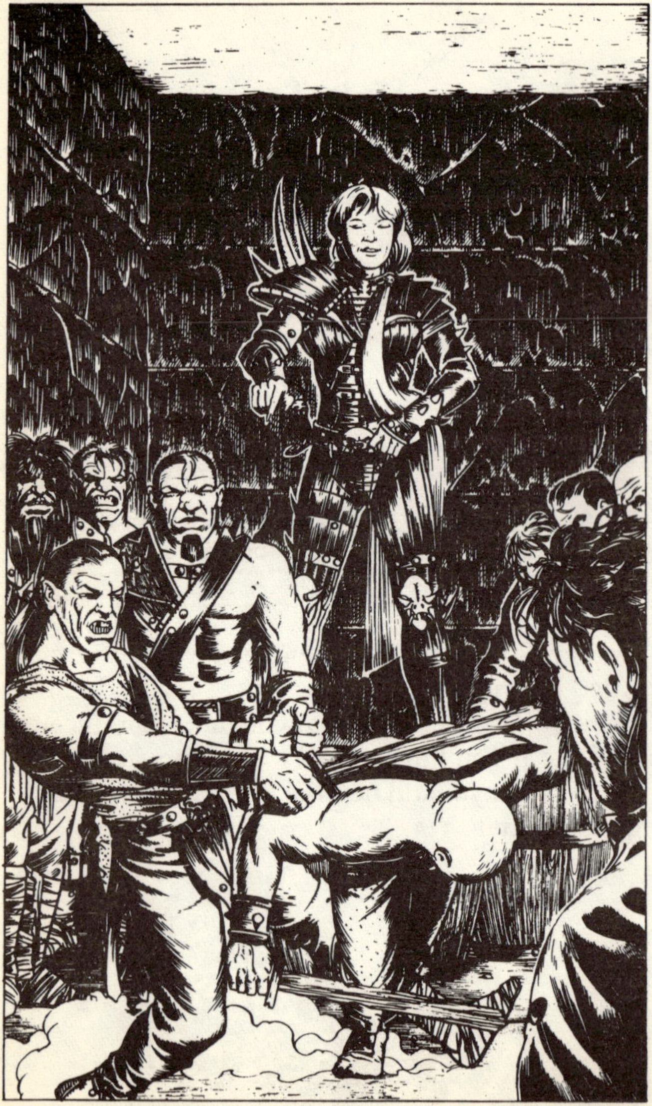

63

The street door opens into a single room in the centre of which two men are engaged in a practice sword-fight with wooden swords. They are being watched by seven other men. At the far end of the room, a striking blonde woman wearing leather armour is shouting out instructions to the two fighters. 'Stop!' she shouts suddenly. 'Take a rest while I see what this intruder wants.' She walks over to you and says, 'I'm Max and these are my boys. Do you want to join them or hire them?' You reply that you may be interested in hiring them. 'My boys are the best. 200 Gold Pieces and all ten of us are yours.' Will you:

Pay Max the price she wants?	Turn to **124**
Haggle over the price?	Turn to **255**
Refuse the offer and leave?	Turn to **314**

64

The guards call out for you to stop, but you run on as fast as you can, keeping an eye out for a tavern into which to dash. Turn to **52**.

65

The street turns sharply right and you soon find yourself back at the main entrance-gates to Zengis. Remembering your promise to Lexon, you decide to return to your waiting army. Turn to **113**.

66

You manage to free a hand and stab the brutal beast in its foot with your sword. It roars in pain and, a split second later, you are free and up on your feet. Now you have a better chance against the flesh-eater.

NANDIBEAR   SKILL 9   STAMINA 11

If you win, turn to **362**.

67

The agile Hill Man suddenly makes his move and, before you have time to react, you are knocked to the ground by a flying two-footed kick. You land with your face in the dirt and feel a sharp pain in your arms as they are twisted up behind your back in a vice-like grip. You try to break free, but struggling only increases the pain and you are forced to submit to Vine. Turn to **213**.

68

You come to a wide clearing in the forest in which there is a large boulder. The clearing is strewn with bones and the boulder is spattered with dried blood. If you wish to wait on the edge of the clearing with your army to see if anyone or anything will come back to it, turn to **252**. If you would rather walk through the clearing, turn to **312**.

69

Ten of your Warriors fall prey to the Harpoon Flies, their bodies to provide food in the coming weeks for the maggots that hatch out inside them. Eventually the Harpoon Flies zoom off and you lead your men dejectedly back to the ship. Deduct 1 point from your LUCK. Captain Barnock realizes you are in no mood for early morning chatter and gives the order to set sail upriver. Turn to **188**.

70

The Werewolf catches sight of your charm and becomes frozen to the spot, rigid with fear. Without any struggle, you are able to dispose of the Werewolf with one thrust of your sword. But you find that the guard is dead. The rest of the night passes without further incident and in the morning you lead your army out of the forest, across the new plain. Turn to **323**.

71

The barman looks at you in astonishment, then picks up a wooden club from behind the bar. He storms out from behind the bar, shouting, 'I'm going to teach this upstart a lesson.' You slide off your stool and draw your sword to face the huge brute as the drinkers crowd around to get a good view of the fight. 'Mince him, Fats!' shouts a voice from the crowd. 'Hurry up, Fats, I want another drink,' roars another. Then the fight begins.

BARMAN   SKILL 9   STAMINA 7

If you are first to win three Attack Rounds, turn to **26**. If the barman is first to win three Attack Rounds, turn to **227**.

72

Another half-hour passes and the paralysis starts to wear off. Feeling returns to your limbs and soon you are able to move freely. Turn to **284**.

73

You quickly raise your shield-arm to block the flying dart. The Blog turns to run away, and disappears into the bushes. If you wish to give chase, turn to

171. If you would rather call your troops back to the path and march on, turn to **130**.

74

The fireball crashes into the mainmast and drops on to the deck, killing five of your men. Two Dwarfs quickly smother the fireball with wet blankets, averting a fire on board. Turn to **192**.

75

While your warriors are recovering, you wonder what plans Agglax is hatching; somewhere beyond the Forest of Fiends he awaits you and your army. When your warriors are finally well enough to march again, you decide to go straight for Agglax, so you turn your army east towards the Forest of Fiends. After crossing one of the tributaries that feed the River Kok, you come to the edge of the sombre forest. Dark, twisted trees reach high to form a threatening wall; a whisper of uncertainty runs through the ranks of the army. You break the eerie silence by shouting the order to march into the forest; the daylight quickly dwindles under a thick canopy of leaves overhead. Only the high shrilling of frightened monkeys occasionally wakes the silent forest. After half an hour, a scout reports back to tell you that he has spotted a group of wooden huts, almost hidden by overgrowing vegetation. If you wish to go with ten men to this village, turn to **238**. If you would rather march on with your army, turn to **180**.

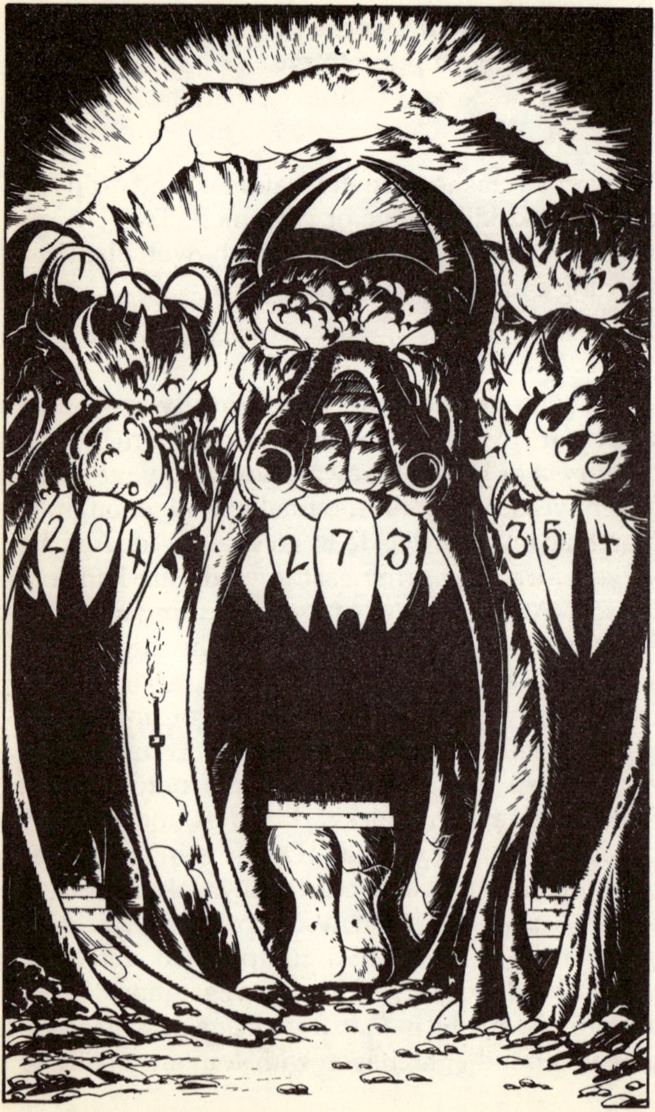
204
273
354

76

The passageway opens up into another cave, although this one is completely empty. However, you have a choice of exits. In the far wall you see the mouths of three tunnels, each one carved to resemble the open mouth of a strange creature, the likes of which you have never seen before. You notice that three of the teeth in the upper jaws of the carved heads have numbers chiselled into them. Choose whichever tunnel you wish to go down and turn to the appropriate number.

77

The old wooden door is stiff and you have to put your shoulder to it to open it. As the door flies open, you hear the piercing scream of a female voice and are startled by what you see. A young Elf is tied to the top of a table, which is bolted to the floor in the middle of the rubbish-strewn hut. Two yards above her stomach hangs a sword, suspended by a single thread of cotton which is looped over the end of an iron spike; this protrudes horizontally from a wooden beam leading down into a hole in the rickety floorboards. 'Don't move!' shouts the Elf. 'One of the floorboards will trigger the release of the sword if you step on it.' You have to decide whether or not to save the Elf. Will you:

Run in to grab the sword?	Turn to **154**
Throw your backpack at the sword?	Turn to **205**
Leave the Elf and march on?	Turn to **320**

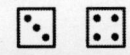

78

You set off quickly down the street before attracting the attention of anybody else. You feel a lump inside your clothing and suddenly remember the leather pouch. You take it out and untie the cord that is keeping it closed. Turning it upside down, you shake the contents out on to your hand, and are alarmed to discover a scorpion on your palm. *Test your Luck*. If you are Lucky, turn to **253**. If you are Unlucky, turn to **240**.

79

Sensing that you are in trouble, Agglax prepares for his moment of triumph. Turn to **301**.

80

The bluebottle hesitates for a second before scurrying on to the jam that you chose. Add 1 point to your LUCK. The man unclips his brooch and hands it to you without saying a word, his face remaining expressionless. You examine the beautiful brooch, which has on it a fire-breathing dragon shown in relief. You turn it over and notice the number '89' scratched on the back. You make a mental note of the number and pin the brooch on to your tunic. If you wish to ask the rogue his name, turn to **3**. If you would rather leave him and move to another table to sit with the three vagabonds, turn to **18**.

81

'I'm sorry,' he says, 'I do go on a bit, don't I?' He hands you your key and you climb the stairs to your room. Turn to **376**.

82

You avenge the death of your troops with one swift thrust of your sword. You climb down from the tree and call out to your warriors to return to the path and march on. Turn to **130**.

83

Five of your Warriors fall prey to the Harpoon Flies, their bodies to provide food in the coming weeks for the maggots that will hatch out inside them. Eventually the Harpoon Flies zoom off and you lead your men dejectedly back to the ship. Deduct 1 point from your LUCK. Captain Barnock wastes no time and sets sail upriver straight away, sensing your desire to get away from this place of ill-fortune. Turn to **188**.

84

The army marches east along the bank of the River Kok until you reach a major fork. Before you rises a dark wall of trees twisting skywards: the sinister-looking Forest of Fiends. You march north for a while until you come to a safe section of the tributary to cross. There is much whispering among your troops as you march into the forest where the daylight quickly fades under the thick canopy of leaves overhead. Only the high shrilling of frightened monkeys occasionally disturbs the strange silence of the forest. As you penetrate deeper, the trees become very dense and it is slow work threading the army between them. If you wish to press on, turn to **155**. If you would like to send out a scout to find an easier way through the forest, turn to **120**.

85

The floor of the tunnel becomes steeper, and walking up it is quite an effort. But your legs suddenly feel full of running when you see a patch of white light ahead. The air smells fresher; soon you are out of the cave and standing in broad daylight at the mouth of a cave only a hundred yards away from your men. They are sitting in a circle, patiently waiting for you to appear from the cave that you entered not long ago. You call out to them and run to where they are sitting to tell them of your underground adventure. You decide to return to your waiting army without further delay.

But the journey back starts with an unwelcome encounter. You see a dust-cloud approaching and soon hear the sounds of galloping hoofs. Ten hostile Centaurs charge down upon you. You must fight a *Skirmish Battle*. If you win, turn to **299**.

86

The moment your swords are drawn, fifteen Hill Men appear as if from nowhere. Dressed in animal skins and armed with stone clubs and axes, the long-haired men run towards you on their wiry legs, screaming at the top of their voices. You must fight a *Skirmish Battle*. If you win, turn to **340**.

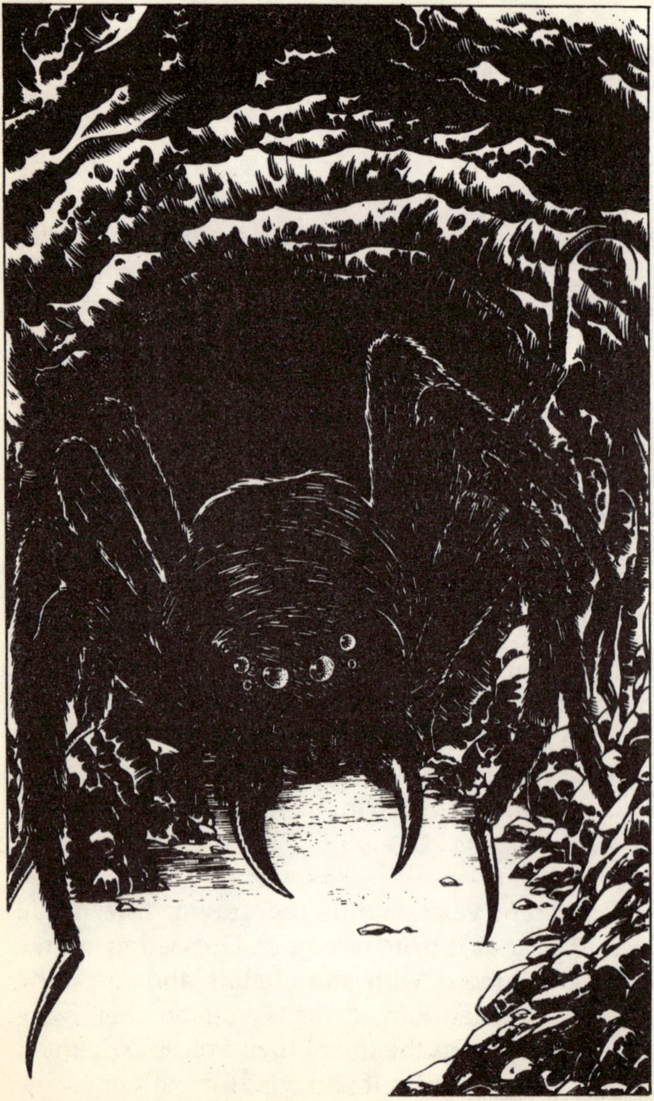

87

As you step into the half-light of the cave, your leg brushes against some sticky threads. As if an alarm had been sounded, a huge hairy spider crawls out from the depths of the cave to ensnare the prey that has stumbled into its lair. You must fight for your life.

GIANT SPIDER   SKILL 7   STAMINA 8

If you win, turn to **275**.

88

You hear a rustling sound coming from behind some thick bushes and suddenly ten huge Goblin-like creatures jump out wielding axes and cleavers. Well over eight feet tall, the brown-skinned Garks rush forward to attack. You must fight a *Skirmish Battle*. If you win, turn to **259**.

89

'Thank you so much,' says the Oracle. 'And now, how can I help you?' You explain that you believe the Oracle can help you to defeat Agglax; you ask if this is true. 'So, you wish to destroy the Shadow Demon? It is good that you have your army with you, as you would never reach Agglax alone. His forces are too great in number for you to slip through them. You must battle your way through to him. You will find a trail of destruction east of the Forest of Fiends. Follow that trail and you will soon catch up with the Shadow Demon's army of death. Even if you destroy his army, however, Agglax will fight on alone. Your weapons will not harm him. Only a void spell will obliterate the Demon. You must find the Crystal of Light. When you are within six feet of Agglax, hold the crystal in both hands and say "Three, two, one – begone." That is how you will rid this land of the Shadow Demon. Goodbye and good luck.' The eyes of the stone face close again and you hear a grating sound behind you. Looking round, you see a section of wall sliding back. Filled with new confidence, you step into the tunnel that is revealed. Turn to **280**.

90

You do not trigger the release of the sword and are able to grab it and throw it aside. The Elf starts to cry with relief as you cut the ropes that are binding her. 'Thank you,' she sobs. 'Thank you for saving my life.' She then pulls a ring off her finger and holds it out to you, saying, 'Please take this ring as a token of my gratitude. It will bring you luck.' If you wish to take the ring, turn to **270**. If you prefer to refuse her gift politely and rejoin your men outside, turn to **211**.

91

Your Dwarfs battle valiantly against the Chaos Warriors but are vastly outnumbered. Refusing to give ground, they stand and fight until the last two of them are standing back-to-back against the fanatical adversaries. Then one of them falls beneath the blow of a spiked mace and the other is speared in the back. Your ears ring with the tormenting cries of the victorious Chaos Warriors. You shout out new battle orders, expecting the Chaos Warriors to attack, but they turn and trot back to their own lines. You decide that attack is the best form of defence and give the order for your army to march on the front line of Trolls. Turn to **178**.

92

'Rubble Street?' Enk continues. 'That's just off the street where we live. We'll take you there.' Unable to think of a good excuse, you agree to their suggestion. You follow them out of the tavern, walk along the street for five minutes, and then turn right into a narrow alley. The three men suddenly stop and turn round, their hands gripping their daggers. 'Rubble Street! There is no Rubble Street in Zengis,' says Enk gleefully. 'Let's get the stranger, lads; those pockets look to be bulging with gold!' You draw your sword quickly as the three vagabonds bear down on you. Fight them one at a time.

	SKILL	STAMINA
ENK	8	7
LAZ	7	7
JIP	7	8

If you win, turn to **133**.

93

The key turns in the slot and you hear a faint click. With a coarse grating sound, the stone slab slides back into the wall and you are able to proceed along the passageway. However, it soon ends at another junction. If you wish to go left, turn to **235**. If you wish to go right, turn to **381**.

94

The Warrior leaves the man to drift downriver to the sea and a watery grave. He swims back to the ship and you are soon underway again. Turn to **234**.

95

On your left you see an alleyway, at the bottom of which is a pile of barrels. If you wish to go down the alley to investigate, turn to **352**. If you would rather walk on up the street, turn to **177**.

96

You come to a narrow part of the chasm where a huge slab of stone has been placed to form a bridge. If you wish to send your army across the stone bridge, turn to **138**. If you would rather march on, turn to **310**.

97

You are consumed by the fireball and are dead even before your troops can reach you.

98

The hole you dig is a yard deep when your shovel strikes something metal. You scrape away the earth to reveal a section of flat iron. If you wish to dig on, turn to **184**. If you would rather fill up the hole again and leave the clearing, turn to **315**.

99

'The Starstone Caves, you say? Yes, I've been there. Dangerous place, full of traps. They were put there by the Oracle, who hates visitors. But the Oracle will speak to most people who can survive his traps and make it to his inner sanctum. It's a challenge, you see. He hates time-wasters. He'll only spend time with people who *really* need to see him, but even then he'll want a few gifts, depending on what information you seek. I suggest you get yourself a guide. Go to Karn. That's about the only place where you'll find one.' You thank the bounty-hunter for the information and walk back with him along the tunnel. Leaving him to collect his evidence from the dead Sewer Goblins, you decide what to do next. If you have not done so already, you may inspect the barrels (turn to **137**) or walk back down the alley and turn left into the street (turn to **177**).

1 2 3 4 5 6 7 8 9 10 11 12 13 14 15 16 17 18 19 20 21 22 23 24 25 26 27 28 29 30 31 32 33 34 35 36

100

You enter a crowded hall which is full of gaming-tables and eager punters. The whole place is buzzing with excitement. You watch a girl spin a huge wheel of fortune and listen to the groans and cheers of the people surrounding her as the number 33 finally stops against the peg. You watch a few hands of cards at various tables, but finally decide to play a game of 'High-Low'. The girl holding the dice tells you how to play. You must roll two dice, but before doing so you must predict whether the number rolled will be 'high' (8–12) or 'low' (2–6). The number 7 is a loser either way. She tells you that you may bet up to 50 Gold Pieces and she will give you the amount you bet if you guess correctly. You may bet only once. If you win, turn to **19**. If you lose, turn to **173**.

101

While taking his axe, you spot a leather pouch on the Axeman's belt; before you have time to open it, however, you see two town guards running up the street towards you. If you want to open the pouch and risk being caught, turn to **281**. If you would rather run off with only the gold ring, turn to **64**.

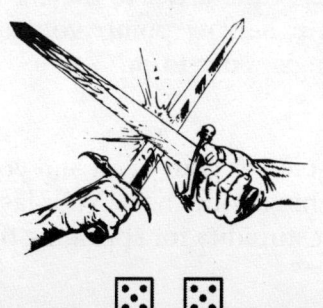

102

The street turns sharply left and then left again and you soon find yourself back at the main entrance-gates to Zengis. Remembering your promise to Lexon, you decide to return to your waiting army. Turn to **113**.

103

You struggle as hard as you can, but you are unable to escape from the vice-like grip of the Nandibear. The brutal beast tears at your throat until you are dead and then begins its long-awaited feast. Your quest is over.

104

Within ten minutes of returning to your waiting army, you give the order to march. After crossing the river at a narrow point, you turn south-east towards Zengis. Turn to **49**.

105

The dagger pierces your heart and you sink to your knees, clutching your chest. Your last thoughts are of your own stupidity for springing the trap.

106

Forty of your valiant troops lie dead or dying on the battlefield. (Reduce the size of your army by this amount on the *Adventure Sheet*.) Trolls are trying to push the brave survivors back, while Goblins and Orcs attack the flanks remorselessly. Berserk with battle-lust, some of the Goblins and Orcs at the back are fighting among themselves, so eager are they to feel the clash of steel. To your right you see a Warrior being attacked from both sides by two Goblins. To your left, another Warrior is being clubbed to the ground by a Hill Troll. If you wish to help the Warrior on your left, turn to **269**. If you wish to help the Warrior on your right, turn to **62**.

107

The barrel lands in the water with a splash and soon floats away and out of sight. Turn to **209**.

108

'Leave no stone unturned when next you come to visit me. Today, your knowledge is lacking and I am thus unable to assist you. Goodbye,' the Oracle intones solemnly. The eyes of the stone head close again and you are left to ponder what to do next. You hear a grating sound behind you; looking round, you see a section of wall sliding back. You have no alternative but to step into the tunnel that has appeared. Turn to **280**.

109

Two arrows find their mark, one sinking into the soft underbelly of the Wyvern, the other hitting the Goblin in the back. It slumps down in its saddle, as the Wyvern continues to climb into the sky despite its wound. *Test your Luck*. If you are Lucky, turn to **24**. If you are Unlucky, turn to **135**.

110

The Rat Men possess no treasure and, after disposing of their bodies, you settle down to sleep, although somewhat uneasily. Turn to **50**.

111

The Hopper makes several peculiar signs with its funny little hands while uttering a strange noise in the back of its throat. Suddenly you are invisible. You clap your hands but cannot see them. A few minutes later, you return to your visible state.

'There's just one more thing,' the Oracle says frustratingly. 'I need a gold brooch. My daughter says she needs one – although I don't know what for, because she is ninety-eight years old. So, if you would be so kind as to give me a gold brooch, I will be in a position to help you.' If you possess a gold brooch, turn to the number that is inscribed on it. If you do not possess a brooch, turn to **297**.

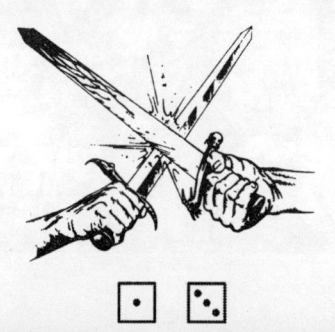

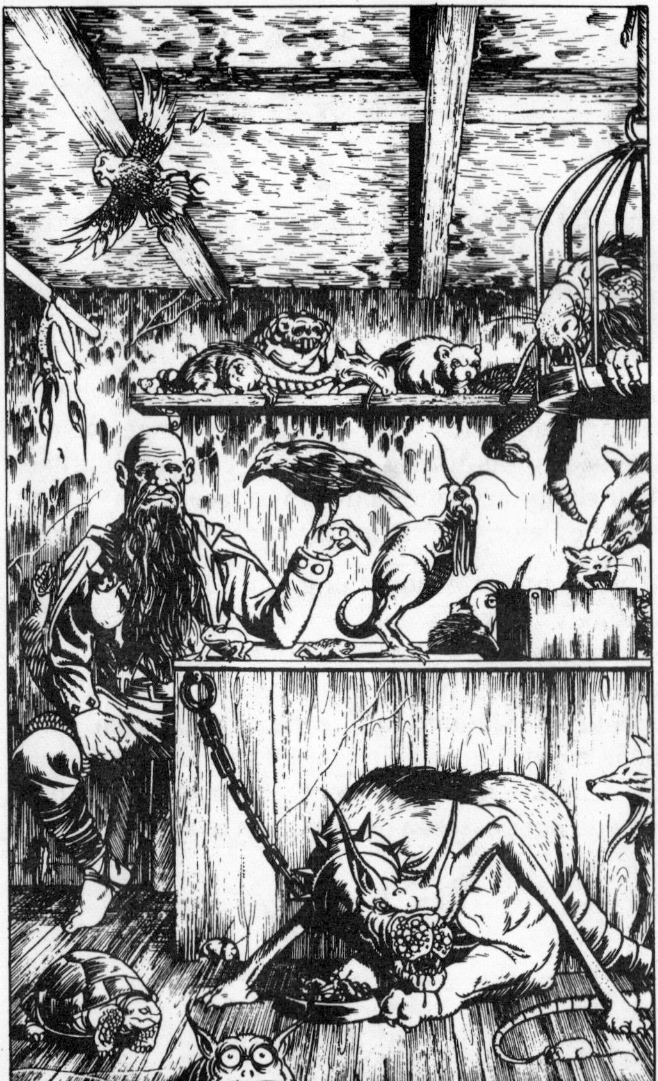

112

As you open the door, a small brass bell tinkles above your head. A thin, bearded old man is sitting on a stool behind a wooden counter talking to a large crow, perched on his hand. 'Who's an ugly boy, then?' squawks the crow in reply, much to your surprise. The old man appears unconcerned at your entrance; you look round the shop and see many small animals – cats, birds and small rodents – and also other, strange creatures. There is one that sits up on its two hind legs like a kangaroo, but it is less than two feet tall and is green and lacks fur. Another is a small winged creature with leathery amber skin; it seems quite content to fly from one side of the shop to the other. Other creatures are equally odd and you are standing looking at them in amazement when the old man suddenly says, 'You are fascinated by my pets, are you not? Are you interested in buying one of them? I have both household pets and familiars that can talk. Some are very special indeed and can even create a little magic. You look like an adventurer to me, so I presume it may be a familiar that you require. Would you like to buy a talking familiar such as my crow here (turn to 47) or would you like a special creature (turn to 369)?'

113

You arrive at the camp before noon and are greeted enthusiastically. You give the order to march. If you wish to cross the River Kok and and march south, turn to 262. If you would rather march east towards the Forest of Fiends, turn to 84.

114

You come to a long, deep chasm which is too steep to climb down and too wide to jump across. If you wish to follow it north, turn to **241**. If you would rather follow it south, turn to **327**.

115

Two hours later, you see a small wood one hundred yards to the north. The Elven Archers suddenly halt and tilt their heads towards the wood, their keen senses obviously aware of something happening. One of the Elves approaches you and says, 'We can hear the cries of several men calling for help from inside the wood.' If you wish to see who is calling out, turn to **28**. If you would rather continue marching east, turn to **295**.

116

The crossbow bolt whistles past your left ear, hitting the wall of the tunnel somewhere in the darkness behind you. Walking on, you soon come to a dead end and find the crossbow from which the bolt was triggered. There appears to be no way of going on, and you have no alternative but to walk back down the tunnel and along the other section. Turn to **85**.

117

You find yourself clutching at air as the agile Hill Man leaps over you. You land heavily on the ground and, before you realize what is happening, your arms are twisted behind your back in a painful hold. You try with all your might to break free but, the more you struggle, the more it hurts. Finally you have no choice but to submit. Turn to **213**.

118

Wielding their flaming swords through the air, the White Knights cut down the Chaos Warriors, despite being heavily outnumbered. When half their number have fallen, the Chaos Warriors turn and flee. Seizing the initiative, you call the rest of your army to join the Knights and march on the front line of Trolls. Turn to **178**.

119

A Warrior dives into the water and swims over to the log. 'He's dead,' shouts the Warrior. 'And there's an Orc's knife sticking out of his stomach. There's also a gold key hanging from his neck on a piece of string. Shall I take it?' If you want the key, turn to **318**. If you would rather leave the man and the key alone, turn to **94**.

120

An hour later the scout returns to tell you that to the south he has spotted a village of wooden huts almost hidden by overgrowing vegetation. He also tells you that the trees are less dense that way. You immediately turn the army south until it is possible to head east without too much difficulty, when the scout tells you that the village is further to the south. If you wish to go with ten men to the village, turn to **238**. If you would rather march on eastwards with your army, turn to **180**.

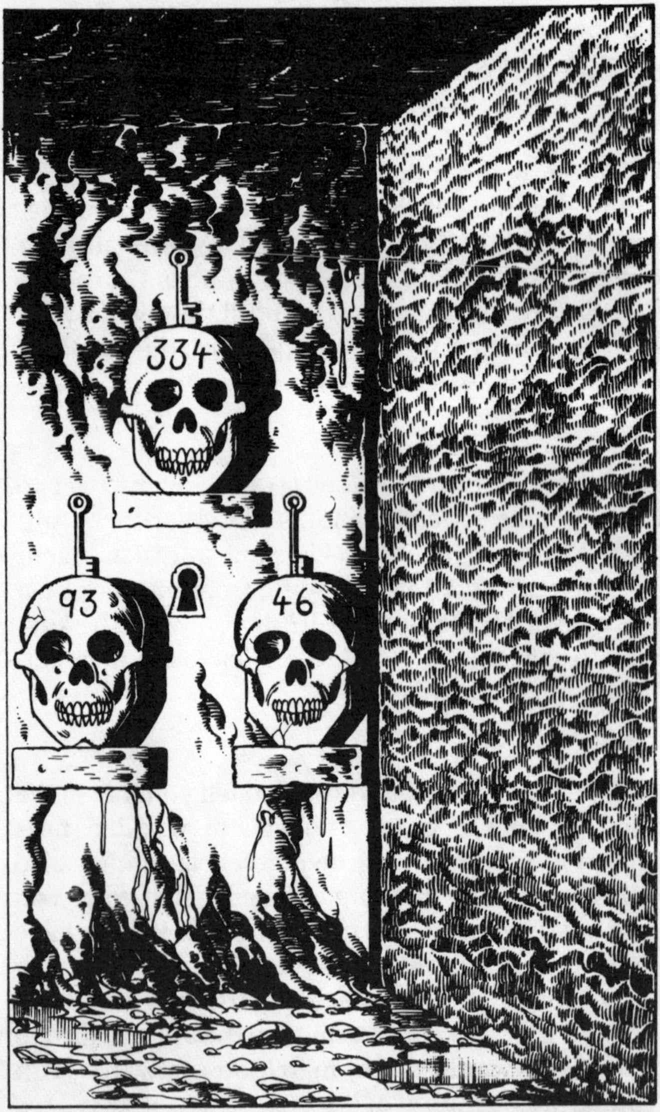
334
93
46

121

A large stone slab blocks your progress down the passageway. However, a slot for a key and a crack between the slab and the side wall lead you to suppose that it could slide into the wall. Three skulls are mounted on stone plinths round the slot, each with a key placed on top and a number stamped on the forehead. If you wish to try a key in the slot, choose a number and turn to it. If you would rather walk back to the junction and try the other passageway, turn to **17**.

122

With a full stomach, your reaction is slow. You feel a sudden pain in your side as the dagger finds its mark. *Test your Luck*. If you are Lucky, turn to **190**. If you are Unlucky, turn to **272**.

123

The Goblin's fall is broken by landing on top of the Wyvern. Although it is bruised and in pain from what you suppose are broken ribs, it is at least alive and may be able to provide you with some valuable information. You walk over to your would-be assassin and ask quite sternly what it knows about Agglax. But the Goblin merely spits at you before pushing a dagger into its own chest. You decide to search through its pockets, and you find a bowstring, five arrowheads and a gold pendant with the number '10' scratched on the base. Keep the pendant if you wish, before giving the order to march on towards Claw. Turn to **220**.

124

You tell Max to go and meet Lexon at your camp outside Zengis where she will receive her payment of 200 Gold Pieces (deduct this from your *Adventure Sheet*). 'You will not regret hiring us,' she says as she leads her men away. You watch her for a few moments, before turning the corner and walking on up the street. Turn to **314**.

125

The Hopper jumps up and down on your shoulder, yapping frantically like an excited puppy. 'No right turns on the way out the caves,' squeaks the Hopper. 'What would you do without me?' You make a couple of facetious suggestions and walk on. Turn to **166**.

126

As you race away, you do not see the Axeman behind you take aim and hurl a throwing-axe at you. *Test your Luck*. If you are Lucky, turn to **371**. If you are Unlucky, turn to **302**.

127

A sprig of belladonna is brought to you and you swallow it as quickly as possible. The belladonna is a poison itself (deduct 2 points from your STAMINA) but, strangely, fights off lycanthropy. The fever soon dies down and you are able to rest and sleep. You feel much better in the morning and lead the army across the new plain. Turn to **323**.

128

For you it will be a long night, a night that lasts for ever. As soon as the moon rises, the amulet becomes animated by the warmth of your skin and the beetle burrows into your neck and severs your windpipe.

129

Fifteen minutes pass by, and still you find yourself unable to move a muscle. Then, much to your horror, you see a head rise slowly out of the sewer access tunnel. It is another Sewer Goblin. It looks first at the bodies of its two comrades then over at you. It climbs slowly out of the tunnel and walks up to you. With one swift movement, its dagger exacts revenge.

130

The path finally peters out at a point where the forest begins to thin. Walking is made easier on the flat, pine-needle-covered ground and you turn east once again. Turn to **114**.

131

The fireball crashes on to the deck, killing five of your men. Others rush to put out the fire before it can gain a hold, and soon it is under control. Turn to **21**.

132

'No exit permit, no exit,' shouts the Calacorm as it reaches for its spear. Now you must defend yourself.

CALACORM   SKILL 9   STAMINA 8

If you win, turn to 377.

133

You rummage hastily through the pockets of the vagabonds and find 10 Gold Pieces and a glass phial containing a green, odourless liquid. If you wish to drink the green liquid, turn to 264. If you would rather leave it, take the gold and go back into the street to explore Zengis further, turn to 382.

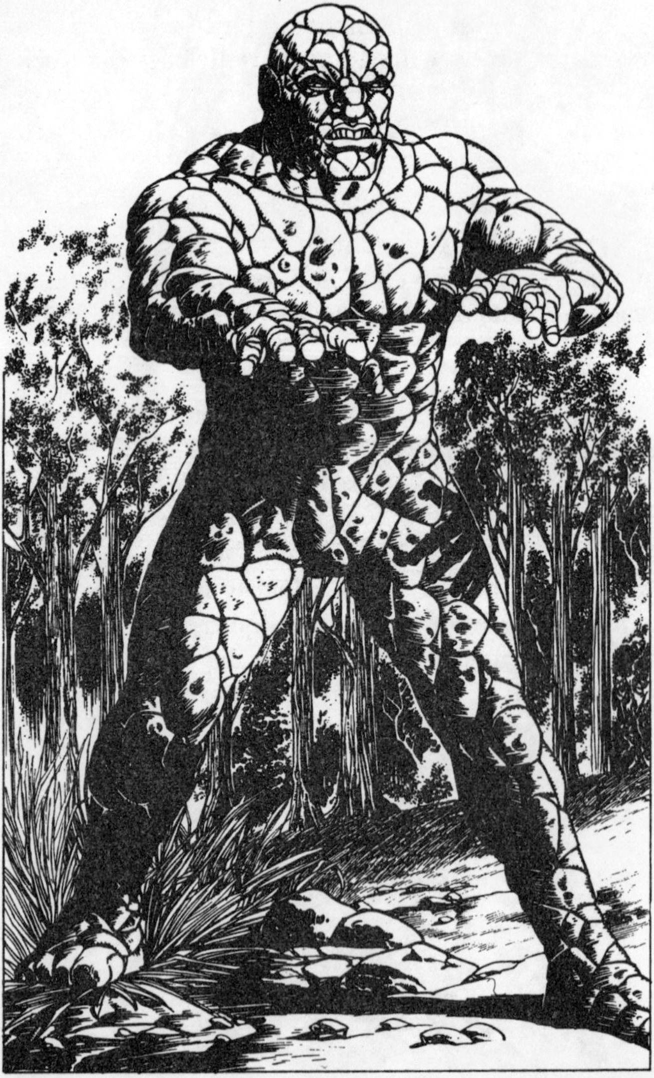

134

A large rock in front of you suddenly moves. Then you realize that it is not a rock, but the back of a Rock Man. It stands awkwardly on its rocky feet and turns to face you. Like a tall man with rough, rock-like skin, the waiting servant of Agglax stretches out to grab you and squeeze the life out of your body.

ROCK MAN   SKILL 10   STAMINA 6

If you lose any Attack Rounds, turn to **202**. If you win without losing any Attack Rounds, turn to **55**.

135

The Goblin manages to stay in its saddle, and soon the fast-climbing Wyvern is nothing more than a speck in the sky heading for the eastern horizon. Aware that Agglax may send more would-be assassins, you give the order to march on to Claw, but with your troops in much closer formation. Turn to **220**.

136

Your temperature increases and the fever becomes worse as the hours roll by. You slip in and out of consciousness, until your body finally gives in to the deadly virus. Your adventure is over.

137

The first two barrels you examine are empty. The third has a piece of old sacking covering it; before you can even touch it, however, a squeaky man's voice shouts out from inside, 'Go away! Leave me alone! Can't a body get a decent afternoon nap these days?' If you wish to pull back the sacking to see who is inside the barrel, turn to **328**. Otherwise, you can either walk back down the alley and turn left into the street (turn to **177**) or, if you have not done so already, descend into the tunnel to the sewers below the alley (turn to **31**).

138

Ten Warriors cross the bridge before you step on to it. You are halfway across when it suddenly moves under your feet. The slab rolls over and you are thrown into the depths of the chasm. Landing on the rocky floor fifty yards below, you are killed instantly. The slab of stone was a Boulder Beast that had been put there to trap you by the servants of Agglax.

139

By the time the *Flying Toucan* has turned and got under way, the pirate ship is less than 200 yards astern. The gap quickly closes until you are thrown on to your back by the force of the pirate ship ramming the stern of the *Flying Toucan*. *Test your Luck*. If you are Lucky, turn to **384**. If you are Unlucky, turn to **215**.

140

You fall backwards, clutching at thin air, and land heavily on the ground, some fifteen feet below. You are dazed and winded, and a pain in your back prevents you getting up. Through blurred vision you see the Blog above take aim with its blowpipe. The poisoned dart finds its mark and you are dragged off to fill the Blog's cooking pot.

141

You arrive at an old building which looks like a barn, with large wooden doors at the front. A man is standing in front of the doors and there is much shouting and cheering coming from inside the building. You step towards the entrance, but the man bars your way. 'Pie-eating competition,' he says gruffly. 'Five Gold Pieces to go in, and then you can join in the competition against Big Belly Man if you think you can out-eat him. Mind you, nobody ever has, I think I should tell you.' If you want to pay the entrance fee and go in, turn to **217**. If you would rather walk on, turn to **95**.

142

The raging battle continues, but still there is no sign of Agglax himself. No sooner have you drawn your bloody sword from the chest of the Hill Troll, than a heavily armoured Mountain Orc jumps over the corpse to fight you.

MOUNTAIN ORC   SKILL 8   STAMINA 7

If you win, turn to **208**.

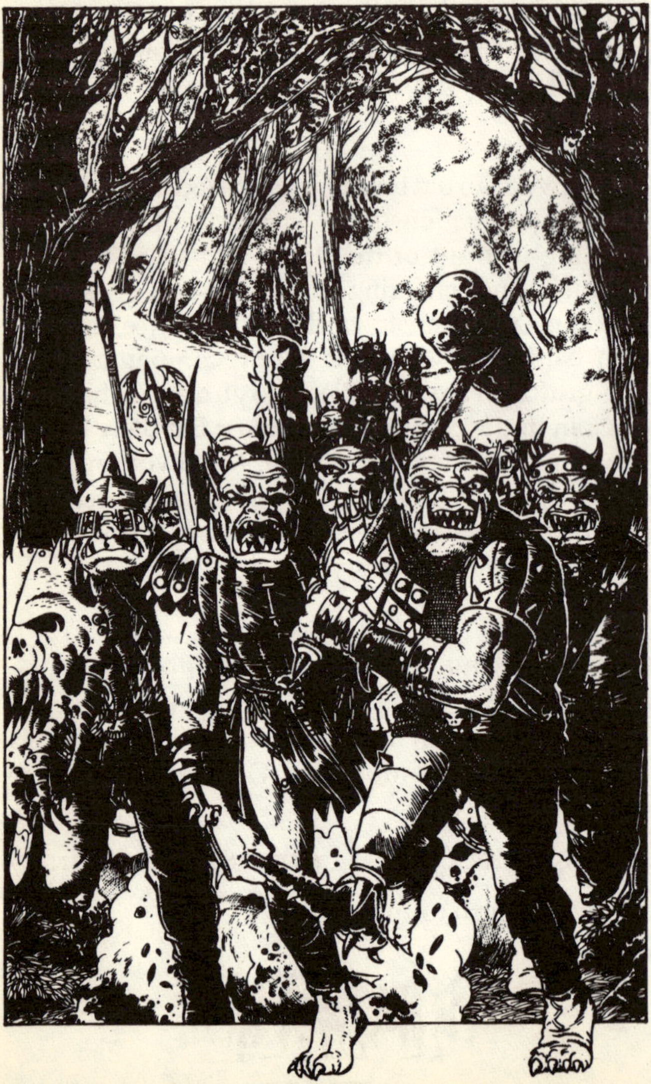

143

You are almost out of the wood when you hear savage war-cries. Fifteen heavily armoured Orcs are running through the trees towards you, brandishing swords, axes and warhammers. You must fight a *Skirmish Battle*. If you win, turn to **242**.

144

'I don't know if you know it already,' continues Thog, 'but the Starstone Caves is a very dangerous, trap-ridden system of passageways and caves, one of which is the hideaway of the Oracle. Even though he has many powers to offer this land, he really loathes all the lying, cheating, thieving, hypocrisy, deceit and all the other bad ways of the beings in Allansia. He will tolerate those who show initiative, however. And if you survive his traps, that will show initiative enough: he'll speak with you. And I'll take you there for 30 Gold Pieces.' You pay Thog his fee and go back with him to the inn.

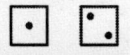

Early next morning you rouse your men and are soon marching south-eastwards. Thog starts to tell you all about his adventures which, after two hours, become extremely boring. Before noon, you give the order to rest for food, just to stop Thog from talking. Even so, he rambles on, spitting crumbs from his mouth while describing the more exciting moments from his tales. Thankfully, you reach the Starstone Caves before dusk and ask Thog to tell you all he knows. 'Two things I should tell you,' he replies. 'Always turn right at every junction. And if you have to choose a number you can see, don't choose one with a four in it. What questions the Oracle will ask you I'm afraid you will have to answer for yourself. You must go on your own and find out.' You wave goodbye to your men before disappearing into the mouth of the dark cave, a lit candle in one hand and your sword in the other. Turn to **219**.

145

A bare-chested warrior dives into the river and swims to the barrel. A rope is thrown to him, and he ties this round the barrel before being hauled up by the deckhands. With a buzz of excitement, the lid is prised off the barrel. But the contents are disappointing – the barrel is half filled with apples. If you want to hand them round to your men, turn to **329**. If you would rather toss them overboard, turn to **107**.

146

As you walk past an alleyway, three dark-cloaked figures leap out of the shadows, wielding wooden clubs. Fight the robbers one at a time.

	SKILL	STAMINA
First ROBBER	7	6
Second ROBBER	7	7
Third ROBBER	8	6

If you win, you decide against going any further in the dark, and you walk back to 'Helen's House'. Turn to **368**.

147

You reel backwards and the arrow thuds into the ground, missing you by inches. The Wyvern is steered skywards again by the Goblin, as your troops rush to you to make certain you are not wounded. You shout at them to fire their bows at the Wyvern, but it is already out of range. As you give the order to march on, you wonder whether the attack had been an assassination attempt on behalf of Agglax. Turn to **220**.

148

The Knights draw their swords, which you see are burning with white flames. Seemingly undaunted by the numbers standing against them, they charge at your troops on their five white stallions. You see them slice through your ranks as the weapons of your soldiers appear to do them no harm. One of the Knights turns his horse in your direction. You raise your sword to defend yourself, but the clash of the Knight's burning blade shatters it into tiny pieces. The Knight strikes again, slicing through your body armour as though it were butter. There you die at the Twisted Bridge.

149

The street continues straight on until you find yourself back at the main entrance-gates to Zengis. Remembering your promise to Lexon, you decide to return to your waiting army. Turn to **113**.

150

The Axeman stands back, cutting a figure-of-eight through the air with the battle-axe which he wields in both hands.

AXEMAN   SKILL 8   STAMINA 8

If you win, turn to **101**.

151

'I'm afraid you are short of luck, my friend,' continues the Oracle. 'Fate has decided that I cannot help you. Goodbye.' The eyes on the carving close again and you are left to ponder what to do next. You hear a grating sound behind you; looking round, you see a section of wall sliding back. There is no alternative but to step into the tunnel that has appeared. Turn to **280**.

152

'I said, go away,' growls the rogue as he pushes the table back and stands up. 'You must be either deaf or stupid. Maybe you can understand this,' he says angrily as he draws his sword. You respond in similar fashion.

ROGUE   SKILL 7   STAMINA 8

If you win, turn to **276**.

153

Standing close by, the warrior woman sees the Goblin just as it is about to fire its crossbow. She dives headlong at you to push you out of the path of the flying bolt. You are knocked to the ground and, when you get up, you see that Max is dead, the Goblin's bolt protruding from her chest. Swearing revenge, you leap to attack the Goblins who are still fighting the surrounded Warrior.

	SKILL	STAMINA
First GOBLIN	5	5
Second GOBLIN	5	6

Fight them one at a time. If you win, turn to **379**.

154

You bound across the floorboards and leap for the sword. *Test your Luck*. If you are Lucky, turn to **90**. If you are Unlucky, turn to **387**.

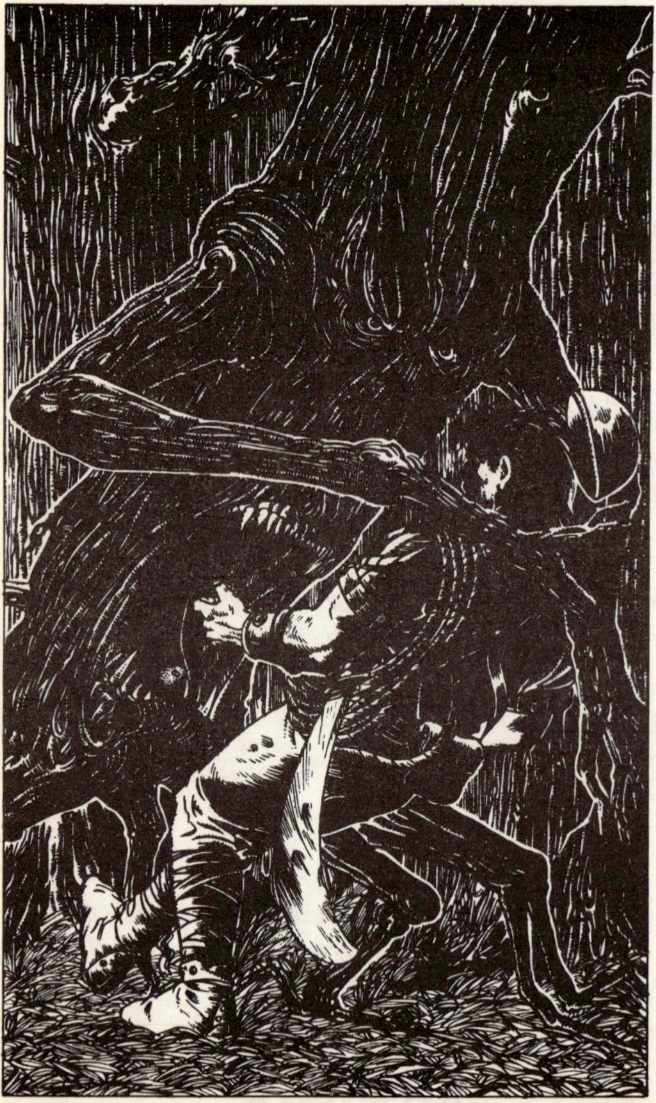

155

The trees become so densely packed that it feels as if they are pressing in on you. You are forced to call a halt and decide to go on alone with a scout to find out whether the forest thins out ahead. Rather than thinning out, however, the trees become packed more closely together until it reaches a point where you almost have to squeeze yourself between them. The scout is walking ahead of you when he suddenly calls out, 'Tree Men!' Just as you reach him, a huge trunk moves slowly forward on its splayed roots and lashes the poor man with its two main branches. All but indistinguishable from the trees around it, you can just make out a mouth hidden in the thick, cracked bark and, above it, a pair of small, ancient eyes which are ringed like the stumps of a branch. The scout is battered to the ground and the Tree Man lumbers forward to crush him under its roots. Ignoring the danger, you draw your sword and attack the Tree Man.

TREE MAN	SKILL 8	STAMINA 8

Both branches (with 8 STAMINA points each) will have a separate attack on you in each Attack Round, but you must choose which of the two you will fight. Attack your nominated branch as in a normal battle. Against the other you will throw for your Attack Strength in the normal way, but you will not wound it if your Attack Strength is greater – you must just count this as a successful defence. Of course if its Attack Strength is greater, it will have wounded you in the normal way. If you win, turn to **290**.

156

The old woman thanks you profusely and reaches out for your right hand with both of hers. 'Let me read your palm,' she says. She opens your hand, pulls it towards her crinkled face and lets out a series of 'oohs' and 'aahs'. Finally she looks up and says, 'You are an adventurer on a very important mission. To fulfil that mission, make sure you drink the Water of the Gods. Death awaits you if you don't.' Without saying another word, she hobbles off and you march south again. Turn to **38**.

157

Your vision blurs even more and you suddenly feel quite sick. You stagger towards the table nearest to you, but before you reach it you collapse on to the stone floor. When you come round, you find yourself lying on a pile of rubbish in a dark alley. Your head throbs with pain and your feeling of nausea is not helped by the foul stench rising up from the rubbish. Thankfully, your sword is still in its scabbard, but if you possessed a pendant or a ring, they will have been stolen from you by the thieves of 'The Black Dragon'. Deduct 1 point from your LUCK. Cursing your decision to come to Zengis, you rise slowly to your feet and stagger out of the alley. Turn to **382**.

158

Your troops become suddenly quiet, then a nervous whisper runs through the ranks. You call them to order and march into the forest where the light quickly fades under a thick canopy of leaves overhead. After half an hour, a scout reports back to tell you that he has spotted a village of wooden huts that were almost hidden by overgrowing vegetation. If you wish to go with ten men to the village, turn to **238**. If you would rather march on with your army, turn to **180**.

159

The fireball lands with a splash in the river, well short of the *Flying Toucan*. Turn to **192**.

160

The glow intensifies as your skin becomes uncomfortably hot. It then begins to burn and you scream out in pain before falling unconscious to the floor. Death by radiation soon follows.

161
You shake hands with the man, sit back in your chair and wait for a fly to descend. Less than a minute later, a large bluebottle lands on the table and moves towards the blobs of jam. Roll one die. If you roll 1–3, turn to **231**. If you roll 4–6, turn to **80**.

162
At last you manage to get round the clearing and head south along the path. Turn to **315**.

163
One of the guards nods his head and says, 'Yes, I saw the army myself, setting up camp outside Zengis. The adventurer must be telling the truth. We'll let you go this time, but don't get into any more trouble.' You breathe a sigh of relief and assure the guards that your only wish is to recruit more warriors. Turn to **78**.

164

Although the ropes creak under the strain, the bridge holds out and your army crosses safely. Heading east, you reach the eastern edge of the forest just as it is getting dark, so you decide to set up camp under the cover of the trees. Looking up at the night sky which is, at last, visible again, you see that the moon is full. You decide to post extra soldiers on watch duty, ever wary of the presence of were-creatures. Turn to **278**.

165

The crowd listens intently as you tell them of your quest; however, unknown to you, one of Agglax's spies lurks among them. A dagger flies out from the sea of faces; you just glimpse it out of the corner of your eye. Roll two dice. If the number rolled is the same as or less than your SKILL score, turn to **293**. If the number rolled is greater than your SKILL score, turn to **122**.

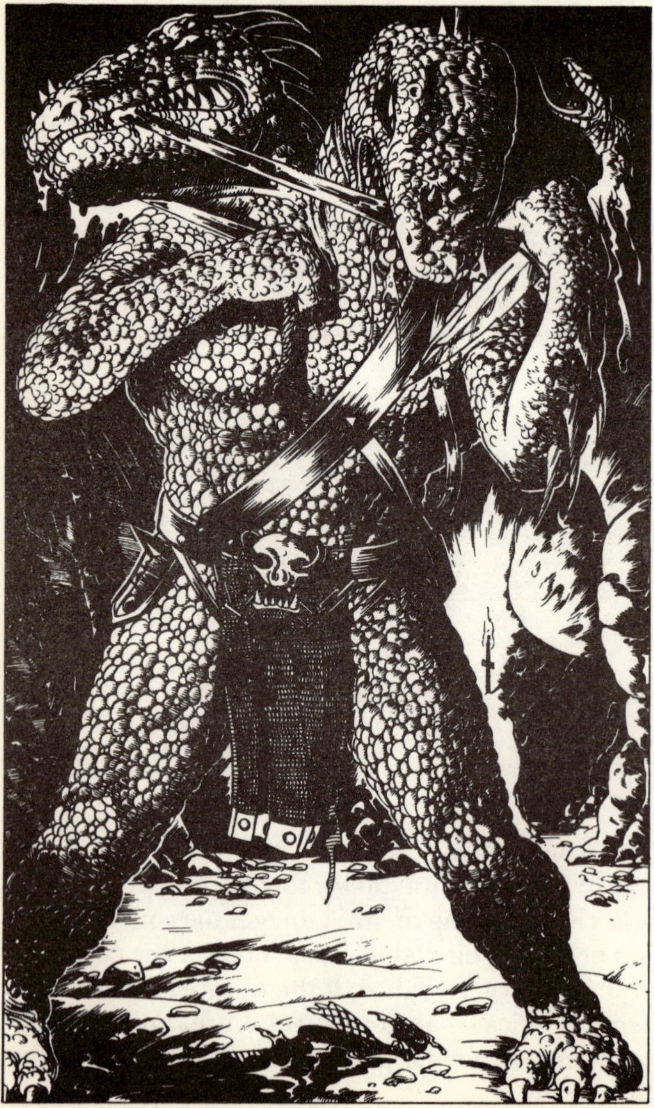

166

The tunnel opens out into a large cave and continues in the far wall. Between you and that tunnel, however, stands a tall, reptilian creature with two heads. It skins a dead snake with its dagger and then takes one bite out of the snake with each head. Armoured reptilians with two heads and an appetite for snakes can mean only one thing – Calacorms! You step slowly into the cave, your hand on your sword-hilt. The Calacorm's heads both start talking at once and you have difficulty understanding what it is saying. Thankfully it takes another bite of snake with one head and continues talking with the other. 'Exit permit must be signed and sealed,' it says to you irritably. Thrusting a piece of parchment into your hands, it shouts, 'Your seal! Give me your seal!' If you have a gold seal, turn to the number that is inscribed on it. If you do not have a seal, turn to **132**.

167

The door is locked and you have to prise it open with your sword. Finally, with a loud noise of splintering wood, the door flies open to reveal a large, rusty iron box. Crudely printed words on the lid give the warning: 'DO NOT OPEN. PROPERTY OF UNMOU.' If you nevertheless wish to open the box, turn to **229**. If you would rather respect the owner's wishes, leave the box and march on, turn to **399**.

168

As you pick the statue up, you hear a click. A dagger with a needle-sharp point is released from a coiled spring inside the plinth and flies towards your chest. *Test your Luck*. If you are Lucky, turn to **365**. If you are Unlucky, turn to **105**.

169

Leaving its hands tied behind its back, you give the Blog a shove with your boot and watch it scamper off into the thick undergrowth. You call out to your Warriors to return to the path and march on. Turn to **130**.

170

A sharp pain runs down your arm from the place in your shoulder where the trident's spikes are lodged. Deduct 2 points from your STAMINA. Gritting your teeth, you pull the trident out of your shoulder. A nimble figure runs out from behind the barrels and dives over the side of the ship into the water, making the quietest of splashes. You look over the side but see no head rise to the surface.

Whoever or whatever attacked you must be an excellent underwater swimmer. You walk over to the barrels and see watery webbed prints on the deck, perhaps those made by a Fish Man. *Test your Luck*. If you are Lucky, turn to **43**. If you are Unlucky, turn to **375**.

171

The nimble creature twists and turns through the undergrowth before scampering quickly up a tree. Will you:

Climb the tree?	Turn to **2**
Chop the tree down (if you have an axe)?	Turn to **257**
Call the troops back to the path and march on?	Turn to **130**

172

You put the mug to your lips and down the foul-tasting drink in one go. 'Ditch water!' you exclaim contemptuously, slamming the mug back down on the bar. The barman sneers, 'The drinks are on me if you can do that a second time.' If you would like to accept the challenge, turn to **249**. If you would rather get on with your business, turn to **40**.

173

'Never mind,' says the girl. 'Come back another time and have another go.' You grunt in acknowledgement and decide to leave the gambling-hall and go back to the inn. Turn to **50**.

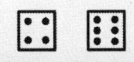

174

'Correct,' the Knight says cheerfully. 'Now tell us why you are marching through this infernal forest.' You tell the Knights about your mission to destroy Agglax. They reply that they would be honoured to join your army, and you readily accept their offer. They also tell you that they know a quick and safe route out of the forest. With the mounted Knights leading the way, you cross over the bridge. By the time you reach the eastern edge of the forest it is getting dark, so you decide to set up camp under the cover of the trees. Looking up at the night sky which is, at last, visible again, you see that the moon is full. You decide to post extra soldiers on watch, ever wary of the presence of were-creatures. Turn to **278**.

175

It is late in the afternoon when the towers and rooftops of Zengis come into view. Captain Barnock appears to relax a little, knowing that he will soon be moored up in the safety of the town jetty. Before going ashore, you appoint a Warrior named Lexon as your second-in-command, and tell him to lead your men to a field outside the town walls and to pitch camp there; you don't want them getting into trouble, and you want them well fed and rested for the next day's march. You tell Lexon that you will spend the night in Zengis in order to recruit more troops and perhaps find out some rumours about Agglax, the Shadow Demon. As your troops march down the gangplank of the *Flying Toucan*, you bid farewell to Captain Barnock. You walk through the main gates of the town and decide to head for the nearest tavern, a place where you might expect to find both warriors and rumours. As you walk down the narrow street between the old wooden houses, you suddenly catch sight of a gold ring lying in the gutter. If you want to pick it up, turn to **292**. If you want to carry on looking for a tavern, turn to **52**.

176

You part the bushes and immediately come face to face with a Giant Lizard. Over twenty feet long, the gape-jawed monster lunges at you.

GIANT LIZARD   SKILL 8   STAMINA 9

If you are still alive after three Attack Rounds, turn to **196**.

177

At the corner of the street, you arrive at a stone building; it has a sign painted on the window in crude whitewash letters which reads 'Max's Marauders – Swords for Hire'. If you wish to enter the building, turn to **63**. If you would rather keep walking round the corner to the left, turn to **314**.

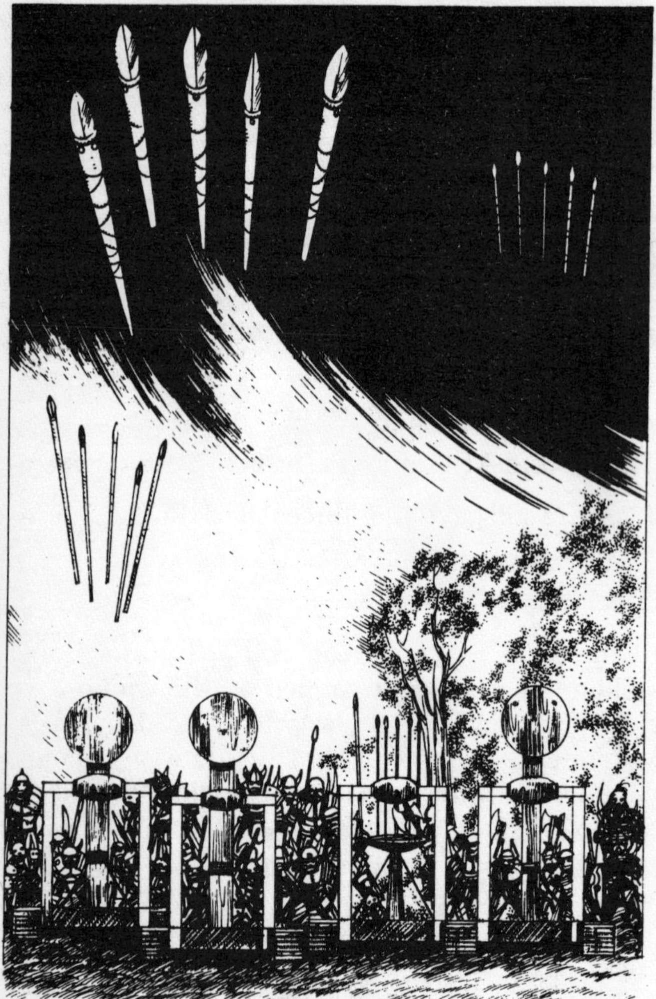

178

As you close in on the front line of Trolls, they suddenly part to allow four wooden wagons to roll forward, each one pushed by crews of shouting Goblins. Your heart sinks when you see the Goblins load large pointed poles into their firing positions, ready to be catapulted at your advancing troops. But there is no going back and you urge your troops on into the mouths of the Goblin war-machines. When you are well within range, you hear their order to fire, and watch the missiles fly towards you. Roll four dice for the number of your troops who are cut down by the war-machines' deadly missiles. Still fifty yards away from the enemy line, your own troops falter in the face of another salvo. In need of urgent rallying, you run ahead of your army to lead them into battle. When you are just twenty yards away from their line, the war-machines are fired again. Roll four dice again and deduct this total from your army. If you now have fewer than one hundred troops in total, turn to **59**. If you have one hundred or more troops, turn to **13**.

179

Half an hour after eating the apples, some of the soldiers start being sick, yourself included. Deduct 4 points from your STAMINA and 1 point from your SKILL. Their health rapidly deteriorates, and two die quite quickly. Before the day is over, fifteen in all have died. Make the deduction on your *Adventure Sheet* and also deduct 2 points from your LUCK. You regret your decision to give the apples to your men and resolve in future not to be distracted from your main objective. Turn to **209**.

180

You pass by a stagnant pool above which the air is thick with hovering insects. In the middle of the pool you can see the corner of a wooden box sticking out of the weed-covered water. If you wish to wade into the pool to retrieve the box, turn to **325**. If you would rather march on, turn to **68**.

181

The path finally ends at a clearing. The trees are less dense beyond the clearing, making it possible to go east again. Turn to **114**.

182

You step out from behind a tree so that the men in the cages can see you. 'Free us! Free us quickly before the Orcs return!' one of them shouts desperately. 'Two days ago their archers cut us down, killing twelve of us and injuring another. We were travelling east to join the army we have heard about that is marching to meet the Shadow Demon's forces.' You sense that the man is telling the truth and instruct the Elves to let the cages down. Ten tired-looking Warriors are freed from their cages, but the eleventh has died of his wounds. The ten are keen to join you when they learn, much to their surprise, that *you* command the army they are looking for. After giving them food and water, you lead them out of the wood. Turn to **143**.

183

The man, whose name you learn is Obigee, goes on at length about a whole series of races, walking round the room and mimicking the antics of the crew. 'Would you like to see a drawing of the crew?' he finally asks (turn to **230** if you would). 'Or would you rather have your room key?' (turn to **81**).

184

You enlarge the hole, to reveal a small iron door which is locked. There is a small keyhole but no key. If you wish to open the door and have a gold key, turn to the number that is inscribed on the key. If you do not wish to open the door or do not have a key, there is nothing else you can do except leave the clearing. Turn to 315.

185

A scream suddenly fills the air; it is made by one of your Warriors and is quickly followed by several more uttered by other men. 'Giant Fire Ants!' comes a cry from an area where there is suddenly much activity: men leaping to their feet and stamping on the ground, and others brushing frantically at their clothing and armour. You order everybody to move out of the long grass as quickly as possible, but when they have reformed by the river bank, five Warriors are missing. You walk back through the grass and find them lying motionless, their bodies covered by the poisonous red ants. There is nothing you can do for them and so you return to your men with the bad news. You begin the march again, although not in such high spirits. Turn to 274.

186

You reach the eastern edge of the forest just as it is getting dark and decide to set up camp under the cover of the trees. Looking up at the night sky which is, at last, visible again, you see that the moon is full. You decide to post extra soldiers on guard duty, ever wary of the presence of were-creatures. Turn to **278**.

187

Only a foolish adventurer would attack a Leprechaun. Before you can even raise your arm to strike a blow, the Leprechaun tosses some magic dust in your face. You are instantly paralysed – the only part of your body that you can move is your eyes; but you still have your senses. For the next half-hour you are stuck rigid to the spot and forced to listen to a long lecture from the Leprechaun on how absolutely wrong it is to attack defenceless people. When the lecture is finally over, the Leprechaun starts to rummage through your backpack and pockets. He takes all your gold items (not Gold Pieces) and says, 'Now let that be a lesson to you.' Then he wanders off. Deduct 2 points from your LUCK and then *Test your Luck*. If you are Lucky, turn to **72**. If you are Unlucky, turn to **129**.

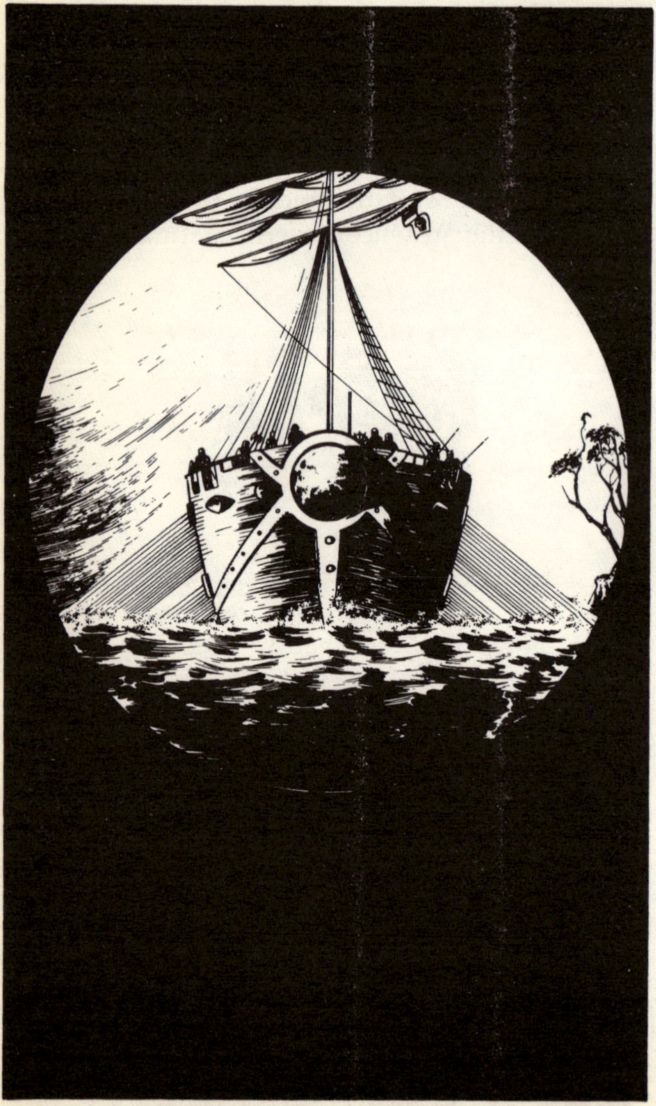

188

Two hours later, the tranquillity of the river trip is suddenly disturbed by a shout from the crow's nest of 'River Pirates! River Pirates!' Captain Barnock reaches for his telescope and fumes and curses as he focuses on the ship coming downriver at full speed. He hands you the telescope and you see the reason for his concern. The pirate ship is of the type built by Northmen, exceptionally sturdy and with a huge iron ramming-spike protruding from the bow. Double rows of oars extend from each side of the ship, giving added speed; the *Flying Toucan* is obviously no match for the pirate ship, which steers a ramming course. Captain Barnock starts to fluster, not knowing what to do. Will you:

Order him to raise a flag of surrender?	Turn to 277
Turn the *Flying Toucan* towards the north bank?	Turn to 353
Order the *Flying Toucan* to turn about and out-run the pirate ship?	Turn to 139

189

You shrug your shoulders in exasperation and trudge back to your troops to give the order to march on. Turn to 130.

190

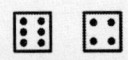

The dagger lodges in the fleshy part of your left side and the wound is not very serious. Deduct 2 points from your STAMINA. As you clutch your wound, a dark, hooded figure slips out of the crowd, through a side door and away before anyone can catch him. You tell them not to give chase as there will be other assassins put in your path before you get the chance to meet Agglax. After bandaging your wound, you hire ten Warriors for 100 Gold Pieces and tell them to meet Lexon at your camp outside the town. When you feel you are sufficiently recovered, you go outside again. Turn to **95**.

191

You free the captured Dwarfs and hear how they had been ambushed in the forest while looking for caves to explore for gems. For saving their lives, they offer to enlist in your army and arm themselves with weapons from the Hobgoblins. A search of the Hobgoblins' bodies yields a gold necklace and a war-banner that was tied to a spear. Its emblem is a red dragon holding a curved sword, against a white background inside a gold circle. You pack away the necklace and banner and give the order to march on through the clearing. Turn to **312**.

192

The River Raiders are obviously unaware of the number of soldiers on board your ship, otherwise they would not have attacked with only twenty men. As they draw closer, no more fireballs are released by the catapult and you must decide what to do. If you want to order the Elves to loose their arrows at the Raiders, turn to **380**. If you would rather let the Raiders climb aboard, turn to **258**.

193

You slay two more of Agglax's creatures and then a spear is thrust in your side. The sheer weight of enemy numbers is too much, even for you and your brave soldiers. You do not die alone this day – but, alas, the enemy has won.

194

The nimble-footed Hill Man's reflexes are sharp, and he jumps up in the air as you dive towards his feet. Roll two dice. If the number is the same as or less than your SKILL score, turn to **373**. If the total is greater than your SKILL score, turn to **117**.

195

Max congratulates you on your swordsmanship and accepts defeat gracefully. You tell her to meet Lexon at your camp outside Zengis where she will receive her payment of 100 Gold Pieces (deduct this from your *Adventure Sheet*). 'You will not regret hiring us,' she says as she leads her men away. You watch her for a moment, before turning the corner of the street. Turn to **314**.

196

Nearby Dwarfs run to help you and quickly slay the reptilian monster. Wondering what other dangers await you in the forest, you march along the path. Turn to **15**.

197

You squeeze between the tables and sit down on a high stool at the far end of the bar. The barman is a huge, ugly brute – if he said his father was an Ogre, you would believe him. 'What's yer poison?' he grunts, to which you reply, 'A mug of apple juice.' 'Apple juice!' roars the barman out loud. 'Apple juice! Ha, the young squib wants apple juice! And I suppose you'll want milk if we don't have apple juice?' laughs the barman as his customers look round to see who he is mocking. 'Well you've come to the wrong place,' he continues. 'We only serve Devil's Brew here. Do you think you can take a pint of that?' If you wish to drink a pint of Devil's Brew, turn to **172**. If you still insist on apple juice and at the same time would like to tell the barman to mind his manners, turn to **71**.

198

Less than a minute later, you hear the Elf scream and a bellowing roar from a huge creature. There is a brief scuffle and then silence. The next sound you hear is that of teeth crunching and gnawing through bone. Some terrible subterranean beast is devouring the poor Elf. His fellow Elves look at you accusingly and you have to feel responsible for the Elf's death. Deduct 1 point from your LUCK. However, there is nothing that can be done for the Elf except, perhaps, to avenge his death. If you wish to be lowered down the rope yourself, turn to **239**. If you would rather leave the clearing, turn to **315**.

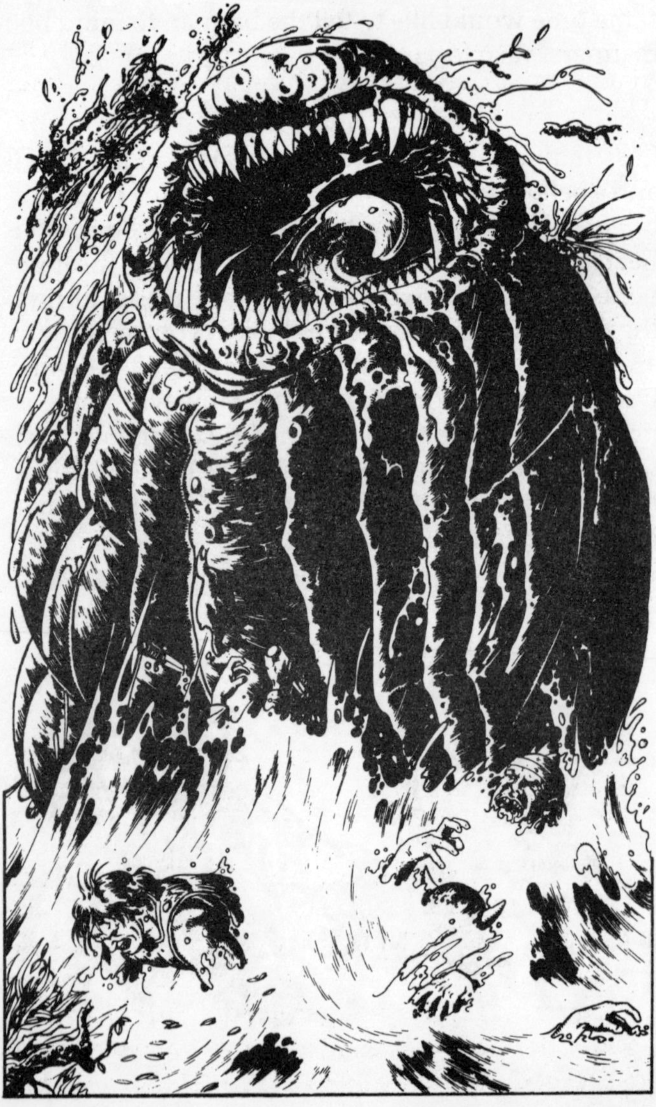

199

It is tiring work, crossing the stinking marsh. The dark brown water rises up to your knees and your feet are sucked down into the black sludge below. You are about halfway across when you see the reeds and weeds ahead of you slowly start to rise out of the water, pushed upwards by some grotesque black hulk. It is a massive creature which breaks the surface of the water, slime and vegetation dripping down the sides of its thick hide, which is lined with deep grooves. A head appears, eyeless and bearing a gaping, blood-red maw lined with rows of dagger-like teeth. It slithers towards you, crushing and drowning five Warriors under its huge bulk (deduct them from your *Adventure Sheet*). The hideous Mudgrinder is almost on top of you and you must defend yourself with your sword.

MUDGRINDER   SKILL 11   STAMINA 12

After five Attack Rounds, turn to **33**.

200

Test your Luck. If you are Lucky, turn to **164**. If you are Unlucky, turn to **34**.

201

'Gladly!' replies the bounty-hunter. He hands you his helmet and you pay him 5 Gold Pieces. The helmet is very solid and will protect you from solid blows that might otherwise have caused serious injury. Add 1 point to your SKILL. You follow the bounty-hunter back along the tunnel and leave him to collect his evidence from the dead Sewer Goblins in the alley. If you have not done so already, you may inspect the barrels (turn to **137**), or you could walk back down the alley and turn left into the street (turn to **177**).

202

The Rock Man manages to get its arms locked round you. Two of your ribs crack under the enormous pressure that the Rock Man applies with its powerful arms. Deduct 1 point from your SKILL and 2 points from your STAMINA. The Rock Man squeezes harder as your troops attack it from behind, but its back is almost as tough as stone and the swords bounce off it. You call for a Dwarf to try to splinter the Rock Man with a warhammer. If there are any Dwarfs in your army, turn to **336**. If all your Dwarfs are already dead, turn to **244**.

203

Some time later, Captain Barnock walks over to you and says, 'We'll soon be dropping anchor for the night. Would you and your men like to sleep here on the deck of my ship or would you prefer to find somewhere more comfortable on land?' If you decide to sleep on deck, turn to **12**. If you wish to go ashore and find some long grass on which to sleep, turn to **337**.

204

You step warily into the mouth, expecting a jet of flame to frizzle you or the floor to fall away suddenly. But nothing happens and you are able to walk on. Turn to **53**.

205

Taking careful aim, you hurl your backpack at the sword, hoping to knock it safely on to the floor. Roll two dice. If the number rolled is the same as or less than your SKILL score, turn to **5**. If the number rolled is greater than your SKILL score, turn to **306**.

206

'That indeed is a pity. Perhaps I'll give you one last chance to make amends, or maybe I won't. Let fate decide it. Now where are my dice?' booms the voice of the Oracle. *Test your Luck*. If you are Lucky, turn to **44**. If you are Unlucky, turn to **151**.

207

With quick reflexes, you dive to one side and only your left leg is burnt by the fireball. Deduct 2 points from your STAMINA. You roll over and try to stand, just as the Goblin rider looses its arrow at you. Roll one die. If you roll 1, turn to **304**. If you roll between 2 and 4, turn to **344**. If you roll 5, turn to **147**. If you roll 6, turn to **283**.

208

The noise of battle rings in your ears as you look round to see how your army is coping against the odds. Roll one die. If you roll 1 or 2, turn to **106**. If you roll 3 or 4, turn to **216**. If you roll 5 or 6, turn to **356**.

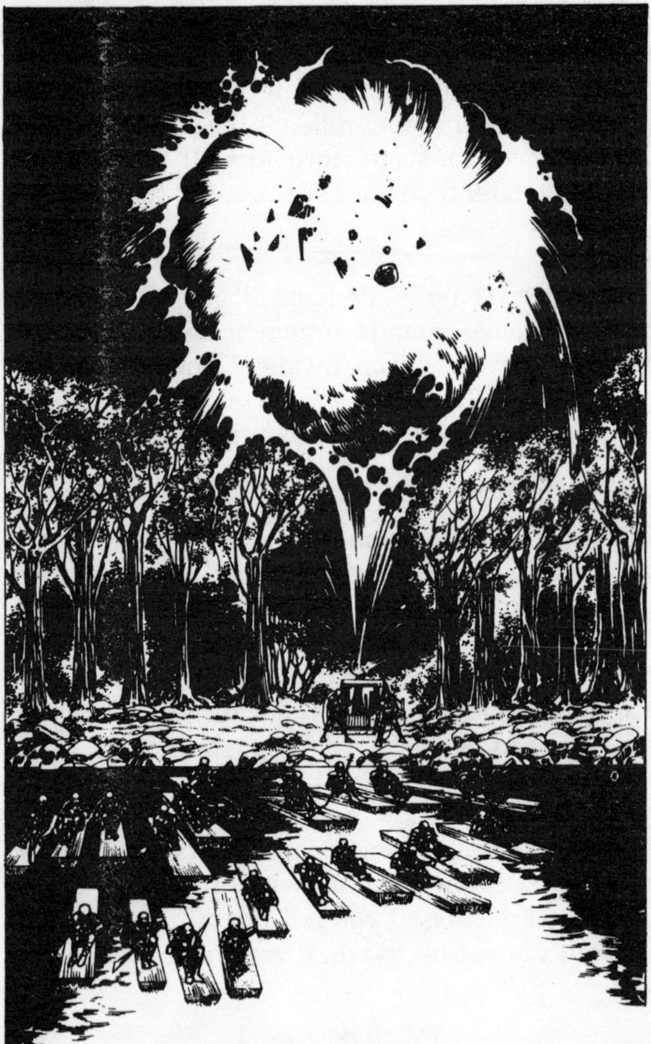

209

As she rounds a bend in the river, the *Flying Toucan* suddenly comes under attack. A large fireball flies through the air towards you, hurled from a wooden catapult that is stationed on the south bank. Under the covering fire, twenty River Raiders jump into their log canoes and paddle quickly over to the *Flying Toucan*. *Test your Luck*. If you are Lucky, turn to **286**. If you are Unlucky, turn to **131**.

210

Time passes by as you slip in and out of consciousness. But at last your temperature falls and you slowly recover. When you finally feel strong enough, you set off once again. Turn to **68**.

211

You continue to march round the edge of the marsh and in less than an hour it is behind you. Turn to **115**.

212

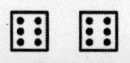

You leave the gambling-hall and make your way back to the inn, but you have the uneasy feeling that you are being followed. You turn to look back but cannot see anybody in the dark. Then suddenly you hear the sound of heavy footsteps approaching quickly and a large figure looms into view. Only when it is nearly on top of you do you see its savage face, lumpy and bestial, drooling spittle down its chin. The Ogre has been sent to repossess the gold you have won.

OGRE   SKILL 8   STAMINA 10

You must fight the axe-wielding Ogre in the dark street. If you win, you search the Ogre, but cannot find anything on it in the dark. You decide to return to the inn. Turn to **50**.

213

Being an honourable person, you stand by your word and leave your ten men to work for the Hill Men. As you leave the village on your own, you turn to wave goodbye to your men, thinking that perhaps they have been saved from a worse fate: a gruesome end in battle against the forces of Agglax. But deep down you know they would have preferred to die in battle and you can't help feeling that you have let them down. Deduct 2 points from your LUCK. Putting the thought to the back of your mind, you quicken your step and return to your waiting army. Within half an hour the army is on the move, heading south-east after crossing the river towards Zengis. Turn to **49**.

214

The tunnel is quite dark and the dim light from your candle does not illuminate the floor. Your foot catches a hidden tripwire which releases a bolt from a crossbow, mounted on the wall at the end of the tunnel. *Test your Luck*. If you are Lucky, turn to **116**. If you are Unlucky, turn to **383**.

215

A rope securing a block and tackle in the rigging above you parts as the pirate ship rams the *Flying Toucan*. The block and tackle crash to the deck, knocking you unconscious in the process. When you awake, you find yourself chained to an oar belowdecks on the pirate ship, the *Flying Toucan* having been sunk. As a galley-slave, you will spend the rest of your days straining over an oar. Your adventure is over.

216

Thirty of your valiant troops lie dead or dying on the battlefield. (Reduce the size of your army by this amount on the *Adventure Sheet*.) Trolls try to push the brave survivors back, while Goblins and Orcs attack the flanks remorselessly. Berserk with battle-lust, some of the Goblins and Orcs at the back are fighting among themselves, so eager are they to experience the clash of steel. To your right you see a Warrior being attacked from both sides by two Goblins. To your left, another Warrior is being clubbed to the ground by a Hill Troll. If you wish to help the Warrior on your left, turn to **269**. If you wish to help the Warrior on your right, turn to **62**.

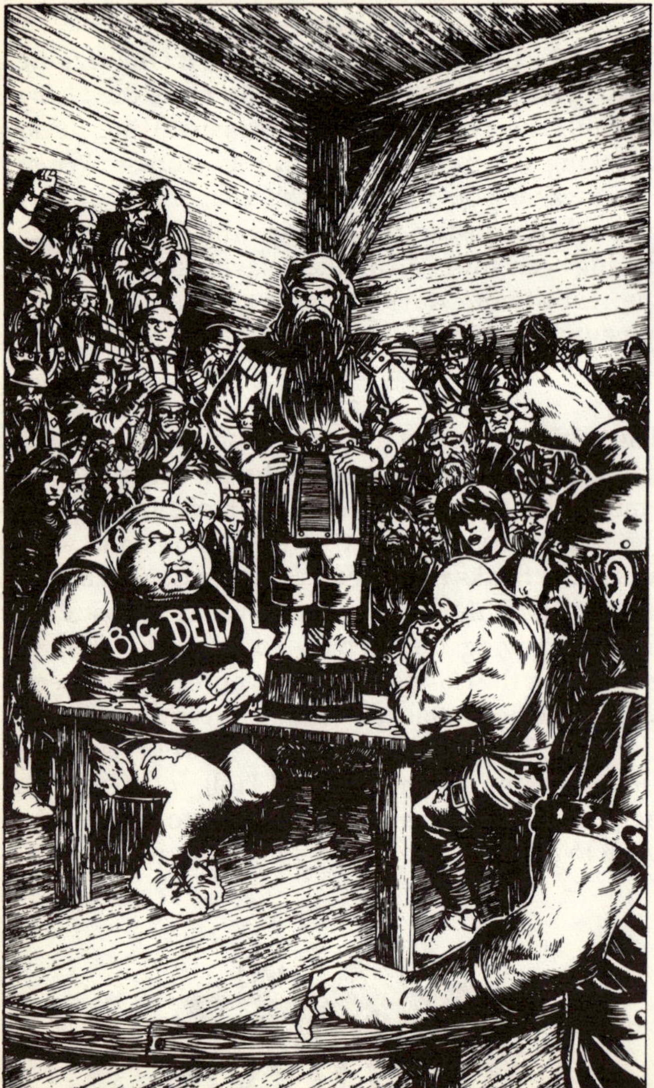
BIG BELLY

217

You pass through the entrance and find yourself in the middle of a packed crowd of cheering people. Some are standing on the floor, craning their necks in order to get a better view of what's happening in the centre of the barn. Others are sitting on the benches of a makeshift grandstand which rises up the other three walls. You squeeze your way through the crowd to find out what is going on, until you come to a circular wooden barrier, inside which two men are sitting at a table, one at each end, gorging themselves on two huge pies. The man to your left is so absolutely enormous that a half-moon shape has been cut out of the table where he is sitting so that he can reach his pie. He is quite old and completely bald, and he has a monocle jammed in his left eye. His gross body looks all the more obese because of the tight black leotard that he is wearing with his name, 'Big Belly', embroidered in yellow letters across it. His opponent, himself a huge Man-Orc, looks small in comparison. A Dwarf, who you are told is the referee, is standing on the table between them, making sure that all the pie is being eaten and none is dropped on the floor. Suddenly, Big Belly Man half-rises and punches the air with both hands, and a loud cheer goes up to celebrate another victory. The Dwarf calls for order and then announces the result. 'Ladies and gen'lemen, the winner of the rat-and-turnip-pie-eating competition is Big Belly Man!' Another cheer echoes through the room before the Dwarf can continue. When the noise has died down he proclaims, 'After a five-minute interval, Big Belly Man will challenge anybody to a fish-and-custard-pie-eating competition. All challengers, sign up here, please.' If you want to enter the competition, turn to **14**. If you would rather leave, turn to **95**.

218

Further along the street, you come to another shop. The window is full of old things, all piled one on top of another: boxes, tins, clothes, tools, pottery, carvings and curios are all heaped up like a pile of jumble. A pawnbroker's sign, somewhat the worse for wear, hangs above the door. If you wish to enter the shop, turn to **287**. If you would rather walk on, turn to **141**.

219

The cave funnels down into a passageway which is dark and cold. Droplets of water fall from the ceiling with a loud 'plop' into shallow pools on the floor and occasionally you think you can hear a woman's laugh coming from a long way away. The passage soon ends at a junction. If you wish to go left, turn to **17**. If you wish to go right, turn to **121**.

220

It is mid-afternoon when you see wisps of smoke rising into the air against the distant stark backdrop of Icefinger Mountains, stretching as far east and west as you can see. The Elves' keen eyesight reveals that the smoke is rising from the chimneys of huts in a small village which, you presume, must be

Claw. You decide to enter the village with only ten men to show the Hill Men that you mean them no harm. Twenty minutes later, you enter the village, but it appears completely deserted: not a soul is in sight. Only the smoke which continues to rise from the chimneys convinces you that somebody must be near by. The village consists of thirty wooden huts forming a circle round one large hut, which you assume is either a meeting-place or a hall of worship. You call out but get no reply, and a shiver runs down your back as you wonder if this is a trap. If you wish to call out again, turn to **261**. If you would rather order your Warriors to draw their swords, turn to **86**.

221

You walk safely along the passageway for fifty yards until you arrive at a crude sign on the wall which reads 'GIVE GENEROUSLY'. Beneath the sign is a large wooden box with a wide slit in the lid. Put whatever you wish into the box before proceeding along the passageway. Turn to **76**.

222

The key turns in the lock and you pull the heavy door open. It is pitch-black inside and you are unable to see anything beyond the door. You drop a stone into the darkness and hear it clatter on to a stone floor below. Will you:

Lower yourself down on a rope?	Turn to 285
Lower a volunteer down?	Turn to 25
Close the door and leave the clearing?	Turn to 315

223

'Sorry for asking,' says Enk, looking all indignant. His hurt expression makes you wonder whether the vagabonds are in fact as tough as they look. Perhaps they may have useful information; it crosses your mind to tell them of your mission rather than fending them off with more lies. But can you trust a vagabond? If you wish to tell them about your true mission after all, turn to 395. If you would rather tell them that you must be on your way, turn to 311.

224

The docile creature sitting on your shoulder awakes from its slumber as you tap it gently on the head. Hoping the Hopper will have the powers its vendor claimed for it, you try to recall the numbers that will trigger its invisibility. If you know the number, turn to it. If you do not know the number, turn to 303.

225

You think about Captain Barnock's offer, but decide you would rather march east as you are more likely to recruit more troops on land. You set off and march through the open countryside without incident, following the River Kok eastwards. In the late afternoon you give the order for your troops to rest, and let them sit down in the knee-high grass. *Test your Luck.* If you are Lucky, turn to **58**. If you are Unlucky, turn to **185**.

226

When you pick the doll up, red gas seeps out of its mouth and forms the word 'Agglax' in the air. Instinctively you drop the doll and it shatters on a rock. Red gas pours from the broken doll and fills the air. It has an immediate asphyxiating effect and you find it almost impossible to breathe. Deduct 2 points from your STAMINA. You order everybody to lie on the ground to escape the gas which is hovering in the air. When it has finally blown away, you find that five Warriors do not get up again (deduct them from your *Adventure Sheet*). In low spirits you march on. Turn to **134**.

227

The third strike of the barman's club hits you on the side of the head, knocking you unconscious. When you come round, you find yourself lying on a pile of rubbish in a dark alley. Your head throbs in pain and the nausea you feel in your aching stomach is not helped by the foul stench rising up from the rubbish. Thankfully, your sword is still gripped in your hand, but if you possessed a pendant or a ring, they will have been stolen from you by the thieves of 'The Black Dragon'. Deduct 1 point from your LUCK. Cursing your decision to come to Zengis, you slowly rise to your feet and stagger out of the alley. Turn to **382**.

228

Test your Luck. If you are Lucky, turn to **364**. If you are Unlucky, turn to **260**.

229

You lift the lid and find that the box is crammed full with the possessions of a Goblin called Unmou. A year-old diary written in Goblin language tells of Unmou's adventures and battles, and this is read out to you by one of your Dwarfs who learnt Goblin during the two years he spent in a slave mine. The Dwarf reads out the last entry with concern in his voice: 'Fiddlesticks barmy, I'm off to join the army! Agglax is yearning for us to do some burning. We're all willing, itching for some killing.' However, you find no map or clue as to where Unmou has gone to join Agglax. His other possessions amount to a blanket, a leather pouch full of teeth, two clay pots, a pair of leather sandals, a brass nose-ring, a pewter mug, a bag of shells, two rats' skulls, a wooden idol and a copper amulet in the shape of a beetle on a copper chain. The amulet is the only thing which interests you. Decide whether or not to place it round your neck before leading your troops north again. Turn to **399**.

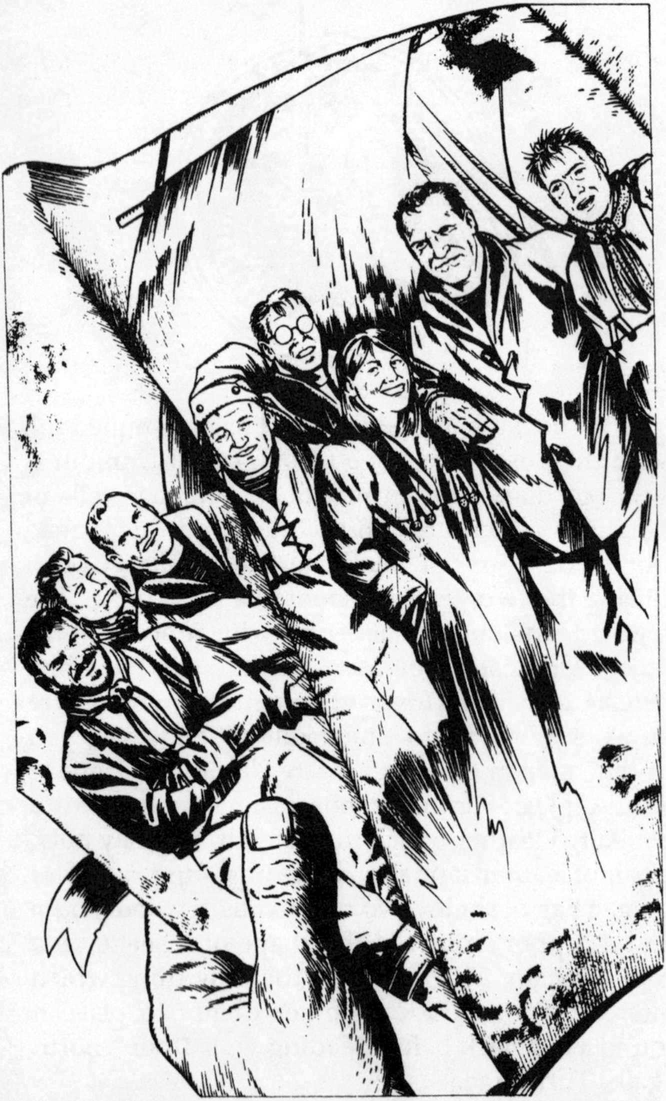

230

Obigee opens a cupboard drawer and pulls out a leather-bound book. He opens the book at a marked page and hands it to you. There are eight people in the picture, each dressed in heavy oilskins. 'That's me,' he says proudly, pointing to the drawing of himself, 'and that's our skipper Preece with the funny hat on. Spike's the one with his hair sticking up, and Euan is the young one going bald before his time. Werewolf's the bearded one, Kwil's son is the one with long hair and the couple there are Klaak and his lass, Welz. Perhaps one day we'll take on Conner himself. He's the best in all of Allansia. Sails in the *Old World* across the Western Ocean, but his reputation is known to all. But that's enough about me, what about you?'

You decide to tell Obigee about your quest and his eyes widen in amazement. 'I'm afraid I'm too old to join your campaign, but I would like to help your cause,' he says before disappearing into a back room. He reappears in a moment, holding a magnificent sword. 'If this cannot slay a Demon, nothing can,' he says with a smile. 'Leave me yours and you can have it.' You examine the sword and see that it is of remarkable craftsmanship; you do not hesitate to make the swap. Add 1 point to your SKILL. Obigee then hands you the key to your room and wishes you goodnight as you climb the stairs. Turn to **376**.

231

The bluebottle hesitates for a second, then moves swiftly on to the jam that the rogue chose. You have lost the bet. Deduct 1 point from your LUCK and remove 50 Gold Pieces on the *Adventure Sheet*. The man drops the gold into his leather pouch, his face still expressionless despite his sudden gain. If you wish to ask him his name, turn to **3**. If you would rather leave him and move to another table to sit with the three vagabonds, turn to **18**.

232

With your sword gripped in your hand, you walk cautiously down the tunnel. The light from the flickering candle grows brighter as you approach it. A figure comes into view and you see at once that it is much taller than a Sewer Goblin: it is a man, carrying a pole-axe and a shield, and muttering to himself. When he sees you emerge out of the shadows into the light of his candle, he stops and says, 'Have you seen any Sewer Goblins come this way?' You tell him about the two that tried to rob you. 'Good. I'll go and cut their ears off so that I can collect my bounty. That's my job, see. Zengis has a lot of trouble with its Sewer Goblins, but not many people like to work down here clearing them out. You did me a favour, now can I do one for you in return?' Will you ask him if he knows anything about Starstone Caves (turn to **99**) or ask him to sell you his helmet for 5 Gold Pieces (turn to **201**).

233
You hear a loud thrashing sound in the bushes off the path to your left. If you wish to investigate, turn to **176**. If you would rather march on, turn to **15**.

234
A few miles further upriver, you come across a bearded man with ragged hair, standing on the north bank. He is dressed in animal furs and is waving his arms at you, gesturing for you to stop. If you wish to sail over to the man to investigate, turn to **298**. If you would rather sail on, turn to **203**.

235
You have walked no more than ten yards along the passage when the floor suddenly gives way under your feet. You have activated a trapdoor and fall head over heels into a sixty-foot-deep pit, where you land on a bed of ugly iron spikes. Pierced like a pincushion, you are killed instantly.

236

Agglax's mouth opens wide as if he is about to laugh, but you hear no sound of laughter. Instead, a jet of freezing gas shoots out of his mouth, enveloping you completely. Within seconds you are frozen to the spot, a trophy for the victorious Agglax.

237

Before he can recover, you lock Vine's arms behind his back in a vice-like grip. You increase the leverage until he sudden cries out, 'I yield!' You let go of his arms and help him to his feet. He rubs his shoulders and says, 'Stranger, you are worthy champion. You now have fifteen Hill Men at your disposal.' Twenty minutes later, after the Hill Men have gathered their belongings and weapons, you set off to rejoin your army, pleased with the knowledge that the diversion had been worth while. Turn to **104**.

238

The group of you walk into the village with swords drawn and come upon the gruesome remains of a number of Wood Elves who have been brutally massacred, no doubt by the servants of Agglax. Looking around, you notice a small bronze statue standing on a wooden plinth in front of the largest hut in the village. If you wish to take the statue, turn to **168**. If you would rather go back to your army, turn to **88**.

239

With a burning torch gripped between your teeth, you lower yourself into the dark chamber. The unseen beast continues to tear at its victim. You run straight down the tunnel and see the sickening sight of a huge, hairy beast gorging on the Elf. Blood drips down its jaw as it looks up in your direction. Swinging your sword, you charge the brutal Nandibear.

NANDIBEAR   SKILL 9   STAMINA 11

If you win, turn to **362**.

240

The scorpion's tail swings up over its head and stabs you with its venomous sting. The poison is quick-acting and you begin to feel extremely ill and feverish. Deduct 4 points from your STAMINA and 1 point from your SKILL. You stagger over to an alley and find a hiding-place behind some barrels, where you can lie down.

Some time later, you wake up and find yourself now able to walk, so you set off in search of a tavern. Turn to **52**.

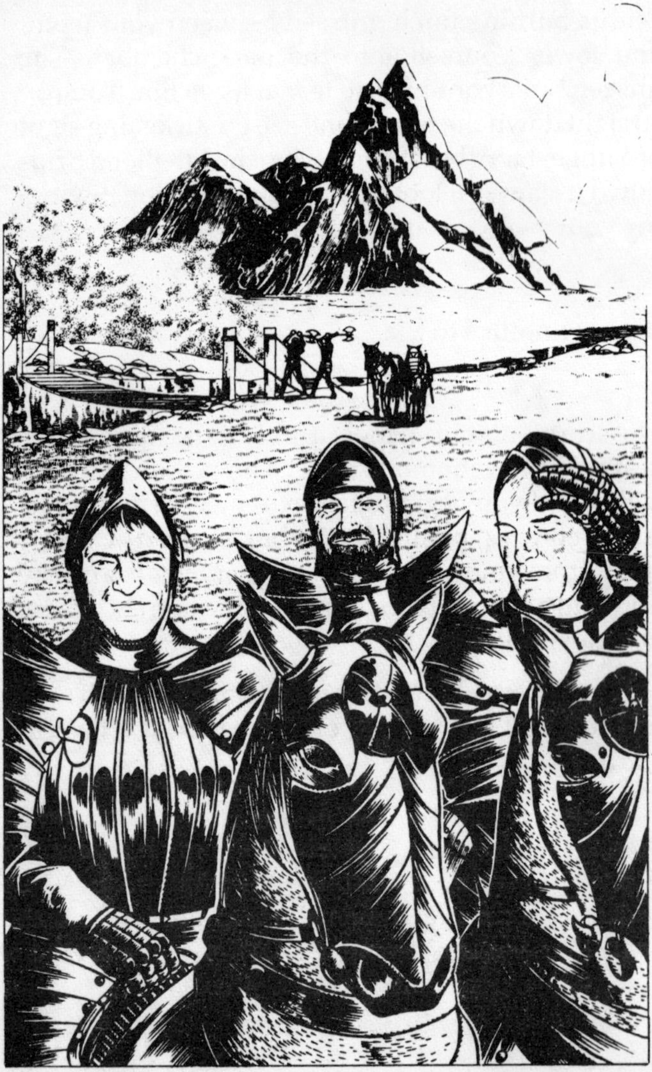

241

Up ahead a wooden bridge spans the chasm but you see that it is guarded by five Knights on horseback. When the Knights see you, two of them dismount and walk to the bridge, each carrying an axe. Poised to cut the securing ropes, they stand with their axes raised above their heads. The other three Knights, still mounted, raise their visors and say in turn from left to right, 'I am Sir Pierce'; 'I am Sir Dean'; 'I am Sir Trevor.' The one who introduced himself as Sir Dean then continues: 'We are the guardians of the Twisted Bridge. If you wish to cross it, you must answer a question.' If you wish to hear the question, turn to **248**. If you would rather attack the Knights, turn to **148**.

242

A search of the Orcs' possessions yields 10 Gold Pieces and some extra weapons for your men. After they have been distributed, you walk out of the wood to rejoin the rest of your troops. Turn to **295**.

243

As you cut the ropes that are tying her, the Elf starts to sob, 'Thank you. Thank you for saving me. I am trained in mental powers and hoped that I could create a barrier that would deflect the sword, but I didn't really know if I could. I would like to have practised first with something less pointed than a sword, but my captors did not give me the chance.' She regains her composure, pulls a ring off her finger and says, 'Please take this ring as a token of my gratitude. It will bring you luck.' If you wish to take the ring turn to **270**. If you would rather refuse her gift politely, retrieve your backpack if you have dropped it and rejoin your men outside, turn to **211**.

244

Warriors drop their swords and pull at the arms of the Rock Man. But its strength is unnatural and the Rock Man increases the pressure on your chest, which is eventually crushed as if it were a tin mug. Your quest is over.

245

After pocketing your gold, the old man hands the crow to you and says, 'Now, Billy, I want you to be a good friend to your new owner.' With the crow perched on your shoulder, you leave the shop. As soon as you are outside, the old man locks the door and hangs a 'CLOSED' sign up in the window. You walk off down the street and decide to talk to your new pet. You ask the crow to suggest somewhere interesting to go. The crow suddenly flies off your shoulder, circles above you and squawks, 'Darkwood Forest! See you there!' Then it squawks again loudly, as though laughing, and flies up into the sky, disappearing beyond the rooftops of Zengis. Suddenly angry, you run back to the shop and hammer on the door, but there is no reply. Annoyed at your own stupidity for buying the crow, you set off alone down the street. Turn to **218**.

246

A silver trident flies over your head and thuds into a mast behind you. A nimble figure then runs out from behind the barrels and dives over the side of the ship into the water, making the quietest of splashes. You look over the side, but see no head rise to the surface. Whoever or whatever attacked you must be an excellent underwater swimmer. You walk over to the barrels and see watery webbed prints on the deck, perhaps those made by a Fish Man. *Test your Luck*. If you are Lucky, turn to **43**. If you are Unlucky, turn to **375**.

247

On a long leash of vine, the Blog walks slowly ahead of you, threading its way between the bushes and the trees. You call out to the other members of your hunting party to go back to the main army and await your return. The Blog quickens its step and leads you to a huge, moss-covered statue standing mysteriously among the trees. It is a statue of an unknown king, standing in a strange pose: one arm is outstretched with a clenched fist, the other is outstretched with a pointing finger. As you step forward to examine the statue, the Blog reaches down for a knife hidden behind the statue and cuts itself free. You hear a noise in the bushes – but it is too late, the Blog has disappeared. You are intrigued by the statue, however, and notice a clean band of stone on the outstretched finger; you assume a ring had been placed here. If you have a gold ring and wish to put it on the finger, turn to the number inscribed on the ring. If you do not have a ring or do not wish to put it on the finger, turn to **189**.

248

'We are the White Knights and we fight on the side of order,' Sir Dean says in a loud voice. 'If you are to prove to us that you also are aligned to order and are worthy of our help, you must answer this question. Which of the three star pupils who trained at the school of the Grand Wizard of Yore was was the son of a priest from Salamonis?' Will you reply:

Yaztromo?	Turn to **174**
Nicodemus?	Turn to **291**
Pen Ty Kora?	Turn to **391**

249

You watch confidently as the barman refills your mug. You put it to your lips and once again gulp down the Devil's Brew without stopping. As you stand up and turn to walk over to one of the tables, the room suddenly starts to spin before your eyes and you see a double outline of everything in your vision. Roll two dice. If the total is the same as or less than your SKILL score, turn to **61**. If the total is greater than your SKILL score, turn to **157**.

250

'You are very observant, my friend,' says the Oracle. 'Now for the final test. I want you to perform some magic for me. You can hear me, but you cannot see me. I think we should be equals. Make yourself invisible!' If you own a Hopper, turn to **224**. If you do not own a Hopper, turn to **108**.

251

You find nothing of interest on the bodies of the Sewer Goblins. If you wish to descend via the tunnel into the sewers below the alley, turn to **31**. If you wish to inspect the barrels, turn to **137**.

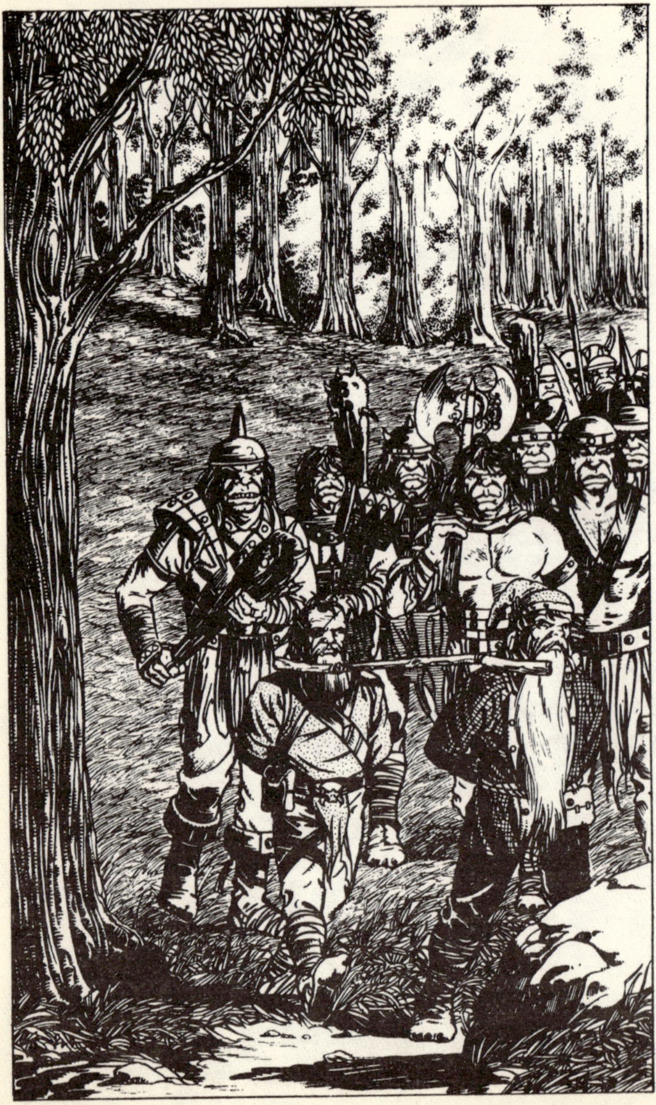

252

Half an hour later, you see some figures walk into the clearing opposite you. Two Dwarfs, their hands bound behind their backs and their necks held by a pole forked at both ends, are being pushed towards the boulder by a group of Hobgoblins. You count fifteen of them in total. One of the Dwarfs is cut free of his neck pole and is then forced to his knees; his head is pushed down on to the boulder as another Hobgoblin approaches with a two-headed axe. To halt the execution, you run into the clearing with twenty-five of your Warriors. Fight a *Skirmish Battle*. If you win, turn to **191**.

253

The scorpion does not sting you, and you quickly shake it off your hand. You think about all the trouble you have already had in Zengis, and you resolve not to be diverted any longer from your plan to find a tavern. Turn to **52**.

254

You run after Agglax and soon catch him up as he scrambles awkwardly across the body-strewn ground in his long robes. You call to him and he suddenly stops and looks at you piercingly in the eyes. You must chant the rhyme to activate the crystal. Turn to the number spoken in the rhyme. If you do not know it or have forgotten it, turn to **79**.

255

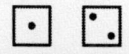

'I'm quite willing to haggle,' says Max, 'but let's decide the price by fighting with these wooden swords. If I land a blow to your chest first, the price will be raised to 300 Gold Pieces. If you strike mine first, the price will be 100 Gold Pieces.' If you wish to fight Max, turn to **41**. If you would rather change your mind and pay the original asking price, turn to **124**.

256

Before you can strike home with your sword, the Mudgrinder suddenly slithers forward. You are flattened by the massive underbelly of the beast and forced underwater. You struggle for a few moments, but then run out of air. Your adventure is over.

257

With your shield held above your head in one hand and your axe in the other, you begin to hack at the tree. Realizing what is happening, the Blog tries to jump across to the branches of another tree. But the branch it catches breaks under its weight and the Blog falls to the ground with a dull thump. Before it can recover, you tie its hands behind its back with a length of vine. You question it about its village and about Agglax; but the Blog understands only a few words of the human tongue and is unable to reply. Will you:

Kill the Blog?	Turn to **29**
Gesture that you want treasure?	Turn to **247**
Set the Blog free?	Turn to **169**

258

You order your men to stand back from the sides of the boat so as not to scare off the River Raiders. Grappling-hooks are thrown up from the canoes, and the Raiders begin to climb up the ropes, yelling and screaming. As they climb on deck, they are greeted by twenty Elvish archers with their arrows trained on them. Ten are captured without a fight before the others realize what is happening and dive into the water to scramble back aboard their canoes. You offer the ten cut-throats the chance to serve in your army or face slavery under Captain Barnock. They have little choice and accept your offer immediately. You relieve their leader of a particularly fine shield and place it on your arm (add 1 point to your SKILL). So, with some unexpected additions to your army (add 1 LUCK point), you instruct Captain Barnock to sail on. Turn to **309**.

259

The Garks' sacks that were tied to their belts are full of worthless trinkets. You soon rejoin your army and press on deeper into the forest. Turn to **180**.

260

Within half an hour of being bitten by the Werewolf, you begin to develop a fever. To your horror you realize it is the first symptom of lycanthropy, the terrible affliction that turns humans into werecreatures. In desperation, you wake all your troops in the hope that one may have some belladonna. *Test your Luck.* If you are Lucky, turn to **127**. If you are Unlucky, turn to **51**.

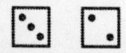

261

Once again you call out, saying that you have come in peace and wish to hire men for your army to fight Agglax. Suddenly a sinewy-looking man with long hair and dressed in animal skins jumps down from the roof of one of the huts, landing about ten yards in front of you. 'I am Vine, leader of the Hill Men. We wish to join your army, but we do not require gold in payment. You must prove to us that you are a true leader. You must wrestle with me. If you win, I and fourteen of my finest men will serve you. If you lose, you will have none, and although *you* will be free to leave, the ten men who are with you must work for us for a month.' If you wish to wrestle Vine, turn to **307**. If you would rather give the order for swords to be drawn in order to show Vine that you have no time for his suggestion, turn to **86**.

262

The army marches east along the riverbank until you come to a wooden bridge. The crossing takes place without any problem, and the river is soon left behind as you march southwards across the Pagan Plain. By late afternoon you have put many miles behind you; you give the order to halt, to enable your Warriors to drink at a watering-hole. Unknown to you, however, the water has been poisoned by one of Agglax's spies and many of your Warriors begin to fall sick. Within an hour, half of them are too ill to march. If you wish to wait for them to recover, turn to **75**. If you would rather head south with fifteen hand-picked Warriors who are still well, turn to **296**.

263

'You are very unlucky, so I am forced to ask you a question that you may find a little obscure,' continues the Oracle. 'I have also been fascinated by the sea and seafaring, and once I met a man called Obigee. He lives in Zengis and works at an inn. Perhaps you stayed there? He loves racing and sails on the *Harem*. Now, here's the question. How many crew sail on board *Harem*?' If you know the answer, turn to that number. If you do not know the answer, turn to **108**.

264

You gulp down the liquid and wait for something to happen. First, your hands and feet start to tingle, then all your limbs seem to go limp. Your sword feels heavy in your hand and sudden tiredness makes you want to sit down. You have drunk a Potion of Weakness. Deduct 2 points from your SKILL, 3 points from your STAMINA and 1 point from your LUCK. Unable to shake off your malaise, you pocket the gold and stagger back into the streets to explore Zengis further. Turn to **382**.

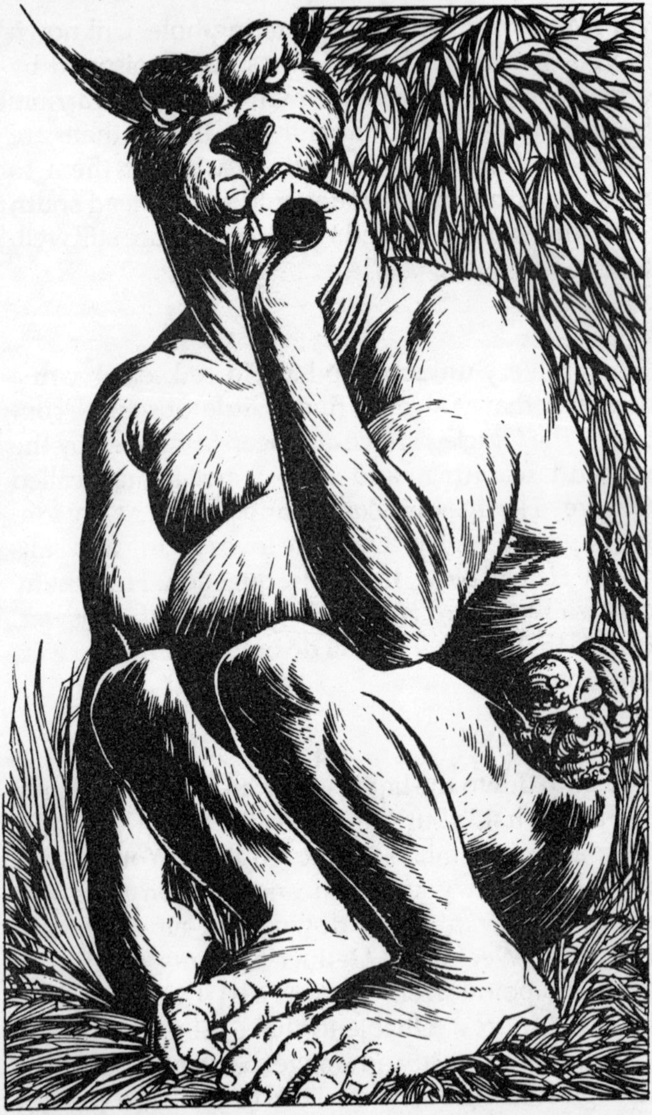

265

You dive into the undergrowth and see movement in the bushes in front of you. Ordering your Warriors to spread out in order to make yourself less of an easy target, you run towards the bush ahead. A small brown-skinned creature suddenly jumps out from behind it, pointing a long blowgun straight at you. You recognize it as a Blog because of its dog-like head and the shrunken heads that are tied to its belt. Infamous for cooking human flesh in large cauldrons, Blogs are hated and hunted down by all human races. A split second later, a poisoned dart is flying towards you. If you possess a shield, turn to **73**. If you are not carrying a shield, turn to **330**.

266

The light is quickly fading as the village of Karn comes into view. The village is a well-known stopover for travellers and is the last human village for many a mile. It comprises some fifty buildings, many of which are taverns, general stores and gambling-halls. You take your men into an inn and tell them to eat well and get to bed early as you intend to leave at first light in the morning. You decide to walk round the village after your own meal. If you wish to enter the 'Blue Pig' tavern to find a guide, turn to **357**. If you would rather go to the gambling-house, turn to **100**.

267
You react too slowly and are struck by a silver trident. Roll one die. If you roll 1–3, turn to **397**. If you roll 4–6, turn to **170**.

268
You soon come to another junction in the street. If you wish to turn left, turn to **338**. If you wish to walk straight on, turn to **102**.

269
Another Hill Troll in the front line of battle picks up a huge rock and hurls it at you as you leap to the aid of the stricken Warrior. If you have Laas of the Northmen with you, turn to **288**. If you do not have him in your army, turn to **23**.

270

You take the ring and place it on your little finger because of its small size. Suddenly the Elf starts to laugh, but it is a sinister laugh. She begins to tug at her ears and you watch her peel the skin forward off her face, to reveal a hideous skull with green, blood-veined eyes. She drops the mask on the floor and steps towards you, mouth wide open. You try to draw your sword, but find yourself unable to move. With terrible ferocity, she starts to bite at your throat, as is the way of a Trickster Hag. Your adventure is over.

271

When you arrive at the jail, the jailer looks you over carefully as the guards explain why you have been arrested. 'Let the adventurer go,' says the jailer, much to your surprise. 'I have heard rumours about Agglax, and I have seen the army camped outside Zengis with my own eyes.' The guards shuffle to one side to make way for you to leave. You hurry out of the jail and across the street towards a tavern that you noticed on your way to jail. Add 1 LUCK point and turn to 78.

272

You slump down on to the table, suddenly gasping for air. You become unconscious and death quickly follows. As the crowd moves forward to see what is happening, a dark, hooded figure slips quietly out through a side door. Agglax will be pleased with his assassin.

273

You step warily into the mouth, expecting a trap to be sprung at any moment. But nothing happens and you are able to walk on until the passage ends at yet another junction. If you wish to go left, turn to **372**. If you wish to go right, turn to **393**.

274

Less than an hour later, the ground becomes soggy underfoot and you see that you are marching straight towards a marsh. If you wish to walk on into the marsh, turn to **199**. If you would rather walk the long way round the marsh, turn to **342**.

275

After wiping the spider's sticky slime from your blade, you take a look around the cave. Hidden among a pile of debris, you find a silver box with a shooting star etched into its lid. The box rattles when you shake it. If you wish to open the box, turn to **398**. If you would rather leave it where it is, go back to the path and march on, turn to **181**.

276

The crowd of people who watched the fight inside the tavern do not look pleased at the outcome. You decide to make a dash for the door before they turn nasty. You run into the street, slamming the tavern door behind you, and carry on without stopping. Turn to **382**.

277

Pirates pay no heed to flags of surrender and certainly have no reputation for mercy. Their ship bears down upon the *Flying Toucan* at full speed, ramming it amidships. You are thrown off your feet by the jolt. *Test your Luck*. If you are Lucky, turn to **384**. If you are Unlucky, turn to **215**.

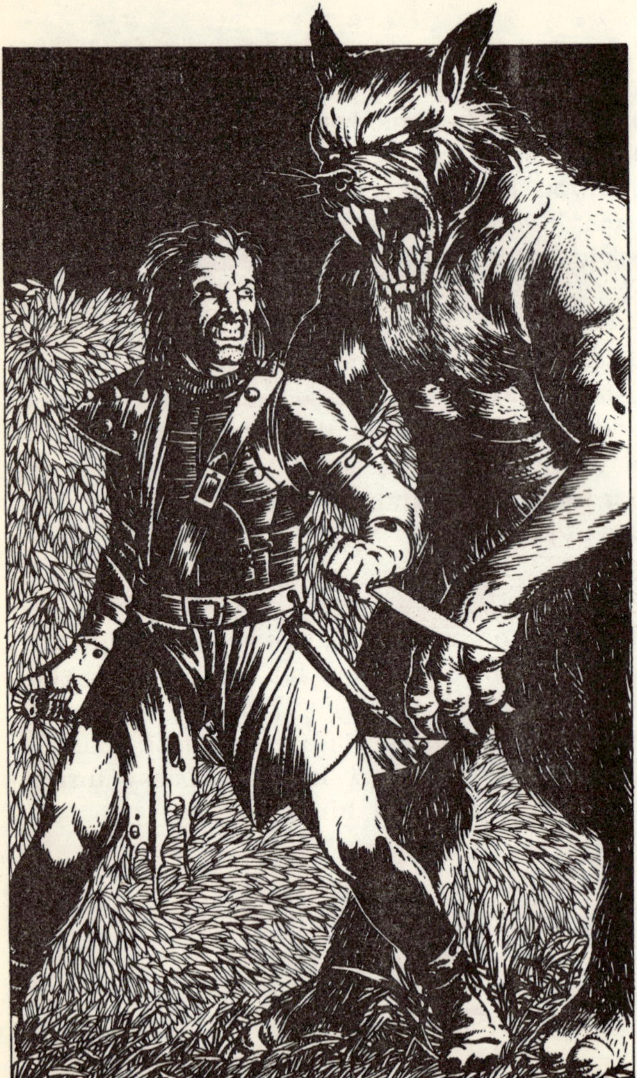

278

Not long after midnight, you are woken by the eerie sound of howling wolves. Unable to sleep, you decide to go and find out if the guards have observed any wolves. You can see some way ahead of you in the moonlit forest and suddenly catch sight of a dark figure moving through the bushes. Creeping up on a guard from behind, the Werewolf raises its head and howls at the dark sky before leaping at the surprised guard. Drawing your sword, you run to his aid. If you are wearing the tooth of the Yeti, turn to **70**. If you are not wearing this charm, turn to **374**.

279

You wake in the morning to a bright, blue sky which completely contradicts the threat hanging over Allansia. Your army is soon on the move again and an hour or so later the towers and rooftops of Zengis come into view. You appoint a stout Warrior by the name of Lexon as your second-in-command; you instruct him to lead your men into a field outside the town walls and to pitch camp there; you want them out of trouble and well rested for the next day's long march. You tell Lexon that you will spend the night in Zengis in order to recruit more troops and perhaps hear rumours about Agglax the Shadow Demon. Promising to be back by noon of the following day, you walk to Zengis and enter the town through the main gates. You decide to head for the nearest tavern, since it is as good a place as any to find both warriors and rumours. Walking down a narrow street between old houses, you suddenly catch sight of a gold ring lying in the gutter. If you want to pick it up, turn to **292**. If you would rather ignore it and head for a tavern, turn to **52**.

280

The wall slides back into place behind you and you feel suddenly trapped as you walk on. Further along the tunnel you notice a piece of paper on the floor. If you wish to pick it up and read it, turn to **343**. If you would rather just walk on, turn to **166**.

281

You cut the pouch from the Axeman's belt and tuck it inside your clothing as the town guards approach you, their spears pointing at your chest. They challenge you; you tell them of your quest and describe how the Axeman tried to rob you. They look at each other, not sure whether to believe you. *Test your Luck*. If you are Lucky, turn to **163**. If you are Unlucky, turn to **324**.

282

You hear terrible screams behind you and discover that five of your Warriors have fallen to their deaths down a pit trap, no doubt dug by the servants of Agglax. Cursing his name, you march on and reach the eastern edge of the forest just as it is getting dark. You decide to set up camp under the cover of the trees. Looking up at the night sky which is, at last, visible again, you see that the moon is full. You decide to post extra soldiers on watch duty, ever wary of the presence of were-creatures. Turn to **278**.

283
You reel backwards and the arrow thuds into the ground, missing you by inches. Six quick-thinking Archers load their bows and loose their arrows at the Wyvern as the Goblin steers it skywards. Roll one die. If you roll 1 or 2, turn to **109**. If you roll between 3 and 5, turn to **9**. If you roll 6, turn to **326**.

284
If you have not done so already, you may climb down into the sewer (turn to **31**), or you could walk back down the alley and turn left into the street (turn to **177**).

285
With a burning torch gripped between your teeth, you lower yourself into the dark hole. You land on the floor of a large chamber in which there is a terrible smell of animal droppings. The chamber is empty but you can make out a tunnel leading off it. If you wish to go down the tunnel, turn to **345**. If you would rather climb back up the rope and leave the clearing, turn to **315**.

286
The fireball whistles by between the masts, and lands harmlessly in the river. Turn to **21**.

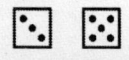

287

Inside the shop you are greeted by a friendly old woman who calls herself Bonny. 'Have a look around, there's a price on everything you can see,' she says in a jolly voice. Two of the walls are lined with shelves from floor to ceiling; they are crammed with more junk collected over the years, most of it covered with a thick layer of dust. You cast your eye along the shelves and pull out several things which may be of interest, each with its own price-tag:

a brass owl	10 Gold Pieces
a copper lantern	5 Gold Pieces
a helmet	10 Gold Pieces
an ivory box	5 Gold Pieces
a green vase	20 Gold Pieces

Buy some, none, or all of these items and pay Bonny for your purchases, before leaving the shop and continuing along the street. Turn to **141**.

288

Standing close by, the Northman sees the Hill Troll just as it is about to hurl the rock. He dives headlong at you to push you out of the way of the flying rock. You are knocked to the ground; looking behind you, you see Laas grinning, his arms still locked round your legs. Quickly thanking him, you leap to attack the Hill Troll, who is still clubbing the stricken Warrior.

HILL TROLL   SKILL 9   STAMINA 8

If you win, turn to **379**.

289

You soon reach the Wyvern and Goblin, but find that they are both dead. A search of the Goblin's pockets reveals a bowstring and five arrowheads, which are of no use to you. Aware that Agglax might send more creatures to kill you, you give the order to march on towards Claw, but with your troops in much closer formation. Turn to **220**.

290

The Tree Man is far too strong to kill, but with its two main branches severed it retreats into the depths of the forest. The scout is not too severely injured; you help him on to his feet and half carry him back to your army. You give the order to head south and, in less than half an hour, you are able to head east again without too much difficulty. Turn to **180**.

291

'You are wrong,' the Knight says sharply. 'Go back whence you came.' If you wish to turn your army round and march south along the edge of the chasm, turn to **327**. If you would rather attack the Knights, turn to **148**.

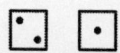

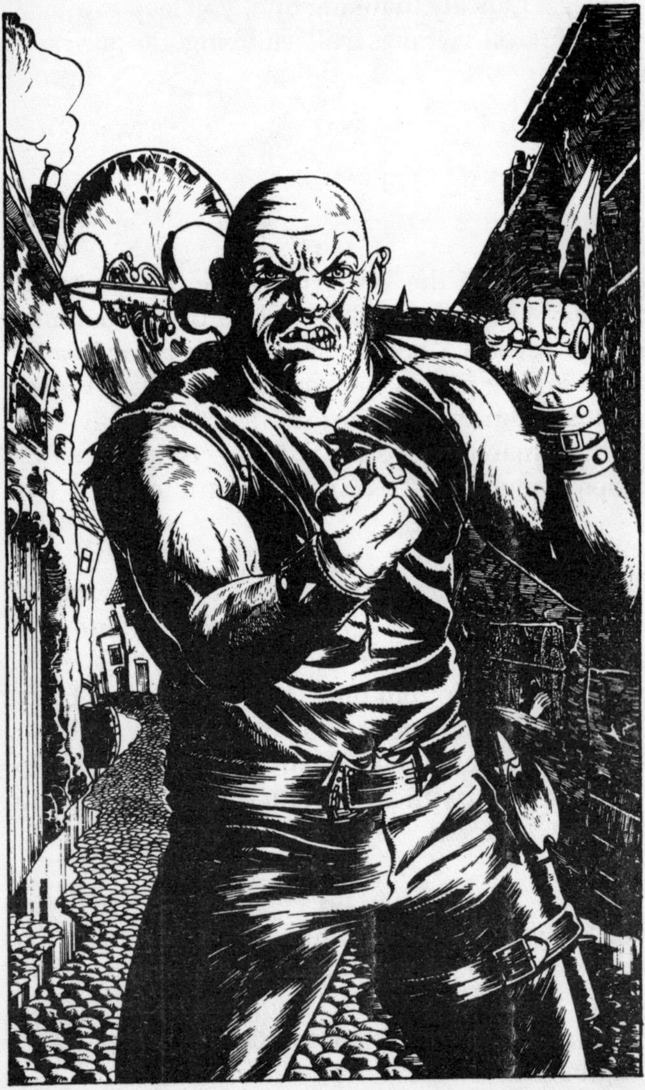

292

You examine the ring and see that it is inscribed with the number '45'. Suddenly you feel a tap on your shoulder; whirling round, you are confronted by a huge bald man, looking angrily at you. An ugly scar runs across his face from above his left ear to the bottom of his right cheek. His bulging muscles stretch his black leather tunic, and you are quick to notice that he is brandishing a battle-axe. A throwing-axe is strapped to his leg. He points an accusing finger into your face and growls, 'That's my ring, stranger. Give it to me or die.' You notice that his fat fingers are far too big for the ring and decide that obviously he is lying. Will you:

Give him the ring?	Turn to 333
Run away down the street?	Turn to 126
Fight the Axeman?	Turn to 150

293

Your reflexes are lightning-sharp and you manage to dodge the flying dagger. A dark, hooded figure slips out of the crowd, through a side door and away before anyone can catch him. You realize that it would be a waste of time to give chase, as no doubt you will have plenty of other servants of Agglax to meet before your quest is over. So you set about hiring ten Warriors for 100 Gold Pieces; you tell them to meet Lexon at your camp outside the town. With your hiring finished, you go outside again. Turn to **95**.

294

You make no sense of the note and, after folding it up and putting it in your pocket, walk on along the tunnel. Turn to **166**.

295

The rest of the day passes without incident; as the light starts to fade, you look for a place to make camp for the night. You soon find a suitable spot by the river and before long a fire is built and the designated cooks get to work spit-roasting wild pigs. Everybody eats well, satisfying their large appetites after the long day's march. After posting six guards for the night watch, you settle down to sleep. Not long after midnight, an owl's hoot wakes you up. The moon is almost full and, feeling wide awake, you decide to go and check the guards. You walk east along the riverbank until you see the silhouette of the first guard, his spear pointing up to the sky. Before you reach him, however, you suddenly notice two shadowy figures climbing silently out of the river. They slip quickly up the bank towards the guard and you see that they are carrying tridents, the favourite weapon of Fish Men! You call out to the guard as you run to help him. As you charge in, you see that the attackers definitely are Fish Men, their scales and bulbous heads unmistakable. You run at the one nearest to you, the guard raising his spear at the other.

FISH MAN   SKILL 7   STAMINA 7

If you win, turn to **16**.

296

Two hours later, you make out a lone figure walking slowly towards you. You can soon see that this is an old woman hobbling along, clutching a wooden stick for support. As you walk past her, she holds out her hand and says in a croaky voice, 'Spare me a Gold Piece.' If you wish to give her a Gold Piece, turn to **156**. If you would rather march on without stopping, turn to **38**.

297

'I'm terribly sorry, but I'm unable to answer your questions as you have failed to please me. Goodbye.' The eyes of the carved face close again and you are left to ponder what to do next. You hear a grating sound behind you; looking round, you see a section of wall sliding back. There seems to be no alternative but to step into the tunnel that has appeared. Turn to **280**.

298

You sail to the north bank to find out what the ragged man wants. As you draw close, nine other men emerge from the bushes but do not raise their weapons. The one who waved to you drops his arms and shouts, 'Greetings, stranger. I and my fellow Northmen have heard of your noble quest and wish to join your army. For 10 Gold Pieces a man we will fight by your side to the death if duty calls.' If you wish to hire the Northmen, turn to **30**. If you would rather refuse their offer and sail on without them, turn to **203**.

299

Two hours later you are back at the watering-hole, where you find your troops fully fit and ready to march. You head east and, after crossing one of the tributaries that feed the River Kok, you come to the edge of the Forest of Fiends. Dark, twisted trees reach up to form a threatening wall. If you have Thog with you, turn to **36**. If you do not have Thog with you, turn to **158**.

310

Twenty minutes later you reach the end of the chasm and are able to head east again. *Test your Luck*. If you are Lucky, turn to **186**. If you are Unlucky, turn to **282**.

311

Not wishing to be drawn into a futile conversation, you stand up and tell the vagabonds that you know exactly where your cousin lives and that you really must be going. Without waiting for their reply, you leave the tavern to explore Zengis further. Turn to **382**.

312

You come across a path that has been cut through the undergrowth. It runs north and south. Will you:

Continue east?	Turn to **349**
Go north along the path?	Turn to **233**
Go south along the path?	Turn to **6**

313

Your losses are bad, but they could have been worse. Five Warriors and five Elves died on board the *Flying Toucan*, and five Dwarfs and ten Knights were drowned in the river, dragged under the water by the weight of their armour. The survivors seem reassured to have firm ground underfoot once more and are keen to start marching. You set off straight away, hoping to reach Zengis the following day. Turn to **366**.

307

As you unbuckle your sword, Vine's men appear as if from nowhere and form a circle round the two of you. Your own men barge into the circle to cheer you on. Vine crouches down with arms outstretched, while his keen eyes watch you intently. He steps to one side, feints a leap and carries on pacing round the edge of the human ring. You follow him with your eyes, trying to stay relaxed, wondering if he will make a move. If you wish to make the first move by diving at Vine's legs, turn to **194**. If you would rather wait and let Vine make the first move, turn to **67**.

308

Your left foot treads on an unseen snake and, not surprisingly, it defends itself by sinking its fangs into your calf. Most snakes in the Forest of Fiends are poisonous, and this one is no exception to the rule. Deduct 4 points from your STAMINA. If you are still alive, turn to **162**.

309

You sail on without incident for another hour when somebody spots a log floating downriver with a man lying across it, face down and motionless, his limbs trailing in the water. If you wish to rescue the man, turn to **119**. If you would rather sail on without stopping, turn to **234**.

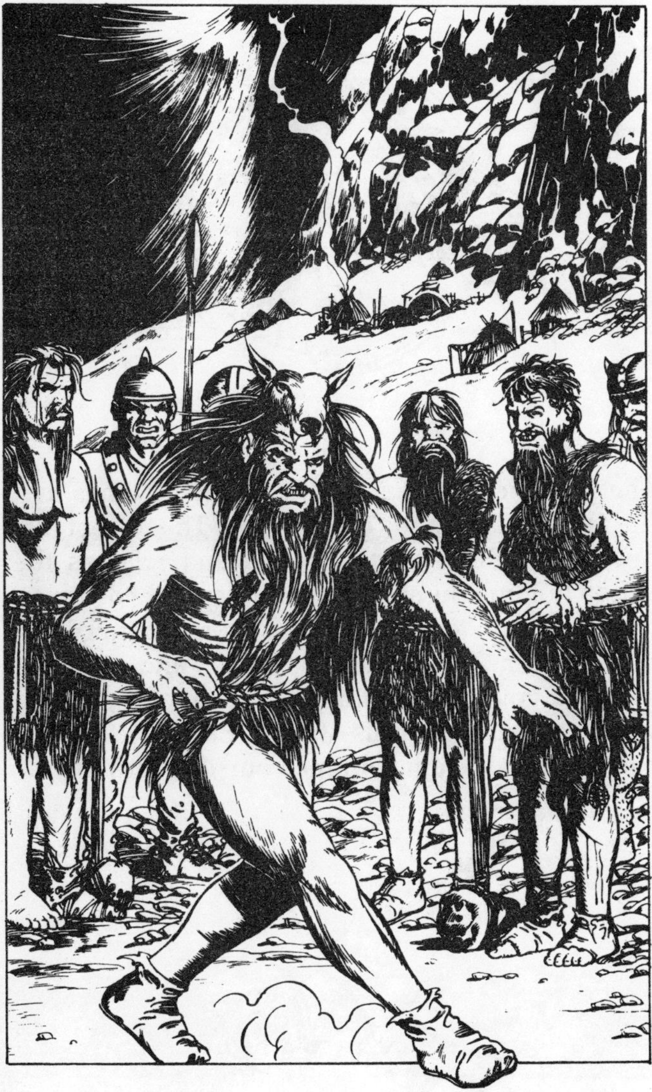

306

The backpack just misses the sword, crashes into the far wall and lands on the floor. The impact tilts one of the floorboards forward and releases the cotton holding the sword. It drops straight down on to the Elf, but, to your surprise, merely bounces off her stomach. 'Untie me,' she begs, 'and I will explain!' If you wish to untie her, turn to **243**. If you would rather leave this strange Elf, retrieve your backpack and rejoin your men outside, turn to **320**.

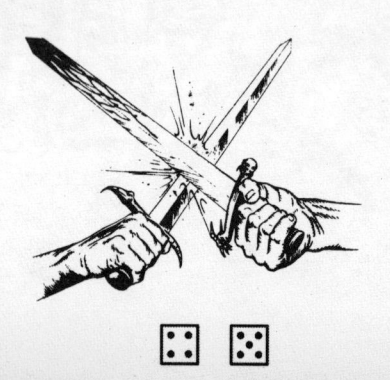

303

Plainly visible, you stand before the stone face shouting numbers. 'You are only allowed one attempt,' the Oracle says solemnly. Turn to **108**.

304

The Goblin's arrow pierces your chest with deadly accuracy at such short range. Your adventure is over.

305

You are fortunate not to have been bitten by the Werewolf, as you could have caught lycanthropy, that terrible disease which turns humans into werecreatures. The rest of the night passes without incident and in the morning you lead your army out of the forest, across the new plain. Turn to **323**.

300

Once back in the alley, you have to decide what to do next. If you have not done so already, you may inspect the barrels (turn to **137**), or you may walk back to the street and turn left (turn to **177**).

301

Agglax's mouth opens wide as if he is about to laugh, but you hear no sound of laughter. Instead, a jet of freezing gas shoots out of his mouth, enveloping you completely. Within seconds you are frozen to the spot, a trophy for the victorious Agglax.

302

The axe hits you in the back of your calf and sends a searing pain up your leg. Deduct 2 points from your STAMINA. Unable to run on, you pull the axe painfully from your leg just as the Axeman catches up with you. He sneers at you, whirling his battle-axe through the air in a figure-of-eight. You have no option but to fight him.

AXEMAN   SKILL 8   STAMINA 8

During this combat, reduce your SKILL by 1 because of your injury. If you win, turn to **101**.

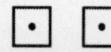

314

The street soon turns to the left again and, as the shadows of darkness start to creep out from the sides of buildings, you decide that it is time to find an inn. One called 'Helen's House' is the first that you come to and it offers rooms for 1 Gold Piece a night. If you wish to spend the night at 'Helen's House', turn to **368**. If you would rather find somewhere else, turn to **146**.

315

As you walk along the path, an uneasy feeling grows that you are being watched. Suddenly you hear a cry from behind; looking round, you see one of your Warriors drop to the ground clutching at a dart lodged in his neck. Another Warrior falls, and you realize that your troops are the target of hidden blowpipes. Roll three dice and add 2 to the total: this is the number of troops who die as a result of the poisoned darts. If you wish to chase your attackers through the undergrowth with ten Warriors, turn to **265**. If you would rather march on quickly before losing any more troops, turn to **130**.

316

The forces of Agglax have had time to regroup while you were engaged in the battle against the Fire Imps. Marching towards you is a long line of Chaos Warriors, their black spiked armour adorned with gruesome treasures from previous battles. Banners flutter above them in the breeze, their red dragon symbol signifying allegiance to Evil. Huge Trolls march behind the Chaos Warriors, with Orcs and Goblins on both flanks, although there is no sign of Agglax himself. The advancing army suddenly stops and the plain falls deathly quiet. Then a small hunchbacked Gremlin steps in front of the waiting forces of Evil and begins to dance and chant. Ending with a piercing scream, he drops to the ground. The Chaos Warriors move forward, treading the Gremlin underfoot. They quicken their pace to a rhythmic trot; the stamp of their feet is an unnerving sound for your troops to hear. Brandishing all manner of axes, spears, spiked clubs and maces, they advance towards you, screaming their war-chants. Arrows will not stop them and you must decide how to fight them. If you wish to lead your Knights into battle, turn to **359**. If you would rather send in your Dwarfs to fight the Chaos Warriors while you wait to see how the battle progresses, turn to **91**.

317

The fanatical Chaos Warriors cut down your Knights until there are only five left standing. You suffer a deep gash in your thigh and a bad cut on your left arm in slaying one of the attackers. Lose 4 points from your STAMINA. With your sword red with blood, you turn to face another screaming warrior.

CHAOS WARRIOR　　SKILL 10　　STAMINA 11

If you win, turn to **351**.

318

The Warrior takes the key from around the dead man's neck before letting him drift on downriver to the sea and a watery grave. The Warrior then swims back to the ship and hands you the key. Inscribed on the barrel you see the number '222'. Making a mental note of the number, you slip the key inside your pocket and order Captain Barnock to sail on. Turn to **234**.

319

'That is a perilous journey,' he says slowly, 'and I'm not as young as I was. But I'd rather have danger than sit around here all day. I'll do it for 20 Gold Pieces. I'll take you through the dreaded forest.' You pay Thog his fee and go back with him to the inn.

Early next morning you rouse your men and are soon marching back to your waiting army. Thog

319

starts telling you all about his old adventures which, after two hours, become extremely boring. Thankfully, you arrive back at the watering-hole where your army is once again fully fit and ready to march. Thog leads you directly east and, after crossing one of the tributaries that feed the River Kok, you come to the edge of the sombre forest. Dark, twisted trees reach up to form a threatening wall. There is much muttering in low voices, but then Thog shouts cheerfully, 'Come on, follow me. It's just a few trees and a couple of monkeys.' As you step into the forest, the daylight quickly fades under a thick canopy of leaves overhead, and the whole place is deathly quiet. 'The creatures are watching us,' whispers Thog, 'but the little ones round the edge won't do us any harm. It's later on when we should get worried. We'll swing right here, to avoid the Tree Men.' Your army threads its way through the dark forest until it penetrates deep into its heart. Turn to **180**.

320

As you close the door behind you, you hear the Elf cursing you loudly for abandoning her. Deduct 2 points from your LUCK; but you convince yourself that your mission must succeed at all costs and nothing must distract you from it. Turn to **211**.

321

A howling scream erupts from the wide-open mouth of the Shadow Demon. White smoke starts to billow from his robes as Agglax stoops in tortured pain. Still screaming, he shrinks to the floor until there is nothing left of him but a smoking robe. Banished to the Outer Planes, never to threaten Allansia again, Agglax is defeated. Turn to **400**.

322

You hand over 10 Gold Pieces to Laz and watch him take out a map from under his robes. He lays the map on the table and you see Zengis in the middle. To the south is marked the village of Karn, and further south-east are the Starstone Caves. To the east of Zengis there is the Forest of Fiends, which starts where the River Kok splits and runs east, almost to the edge of the map. Laz takes out a black crayon and marks a large cross on the eastern edge of the map, just where the Forest of Fiends ends. 'That's where you'll find him,' says Laz. You fold up the map and put it in your tunic pocket. You thank the vagabonds for their help and leave the tavern to explore Zengis further. Turn to **382**.

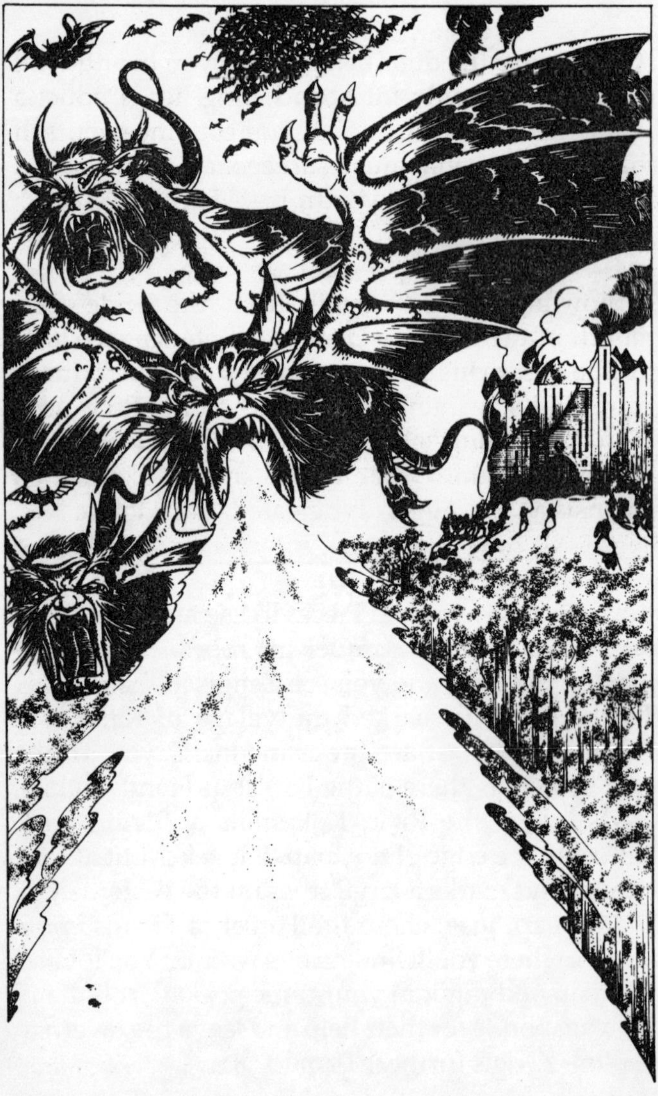

323

The morning passes uneventfully, except for the sighting of a young Dragon with a Goblin on its back. Flying above the range of your arrows, the Dragon circles above your army for a few minutes and then flies back east, no doubt to report your presence to Agglax. You march on, and it is late afternoon when you see smoke rising up into the sky from a burning temple which is under attack from hordes of Chaos Warriors. But as you turn your army towards the temple, you realize that somebody or something doesn't want you to stop the carnage. A small black cloud of flying creatures moves quickly towards you and, as they swoop down to attack your army, you see that they are Fire Imps. No more than three feet in length, they are red in colour and have a pair of horns protuding from their heads and a small tail trailing behind them as they fly. Spitting fire from their wide-open mouths, they are ferocious creatures. They number fifty in total. If you have any Elven Archers left alive, turn to 4. If you do not have any Archers, turn to 386.

324

The guards decide that you are lying and tell you that you are under arrest. If you agree to go peacefully with the guards to jail, turn to 271. If you would rather resist arrest and fight the guards, turn to 363.

325

You are bitten by dozens of insects as you wade out to the box. You pull the box out of the thick, clinging mud and then climb back out of the pool. You prise the box open – and find that it is full of bones which are of no use to you at all. You hurl the box back into the pool and then suddenly you feel quite dizzy. You are forced to sit down, and you break out into a sweat. Your temperature rises and you are trembling with fever. A mosquito has infected you with a virulent form of malaria. Lose 8 points from your STAMINA. If you are still alive, roll three dice. If the total is the same as or less than your SKILL, turn to **210**. If the total is greater than your SKILL, turn to **136**.

326

All six arrows find their mark in the soft underbody of the Wyvern. It crashes to the ground, accompanied by the screams of the Goblin. *Test your Luck*. If you are Lucky, turn to **123**. If you are Unlucky, turn to **289**.

327

A rope bridge spans the chasm up ahead. You order a man across the bridge to make sure that it will bear his weight. He clambers across to the other side and turns to await your instructions. If you wish to send your army across the bridge, turn to **200**. If you would rather call the man back and walk on, turn to **96**.

328

You pull back the sacking and are confronted by a small man, no more than three feet tall; he is dressed in bright green clothes and is curled up inside the barrel. He glares up at you with an angry expression on his angular face. He has an odd-shaped hat on his head that appears to be held in place by his long pointed ears. 'Put the cover back!' he shouts in his squeaky voice. 'I'm warning you.' Then, as if from nowhere, a rotten tomato hits you in the face. As you stand there with bits of tomato dripping off your chin, the small man begins to laugh. Will you leave him alone (turn to **284**) or attack him (turn to **187**)?

329
As anybody in Fang could tell you, a barrel floating down the River Kok is a not unfamiliar sight; it happens at least once a month, and the citizens of Fang have learnt through bitter experience to let it float by and out to sea. The barrels are put into the river by a mad Hag who always poisons the apples first, and this is no exception. Roll one die. If you roll 1 or 2, turn to **179**. If you roll 3 or 4, turn to **367**. If you roll 5 or 6, turn to **54**.

330
The deadly dart finds its mark and lodges in your shoulder. The fatal poison rushes quickly through your veins and its effect is almost instantaneous. You fall to the ground and are dragged off, to end up later in a cooking-pot.

331
You march on until late afternoon, stopping only once for food; but as the light fades you are forced to

find somewhere to sleep for the night. You come across a ruined stone building, perhaps a trading-post of old. A fire is built and you and your fifteen men huddle round it to warm yourselves against the sudden coldness of the dark plain. Above the sound of the crackling fire you suddenly hear the sound of one rock hitting another outside. Quickly, you order your men to draw their swords, just as ten Rat Men burst through the broken doorway. You must fight a *Skirmish Battle*. If you win, turn to **110**.

332

You reach for your seal and stamp it down on the hot wax which the Calacorm drips on to the parchment. After signing your name above it, the Calacorm grunts and says, 'Go.' Without waiting for it to change its mind, you cross the cave to the tunnel. Turn to **377**.

333

The Axeman snatches the ring from your outstretched hand, snorts once in satisfaction, then turns and walks away. You set off in the opposite direction in search of a tavern. Turn to **52**.

334

The key turns in the slot and you hear a faint click. The next thing you hear is the hissing sound of gas escaping from the slot; before you realize what is happening, you have inhaled some. It is a deadly poison and you slump to the ground, clutching your throat and gasping for air. Your adventure is over.

335

You hand over the gold to the old man, who quickly locks it away in a drawer. He picks up the little creature and places it on your shoulder, saying, 'Now, Roob, be a good friend to your new owner. Remember everything I taught you.' With the Hopper sitting happily on your shoulder, you walk out of the shop and on up the street. Turn to **218**.

336

A Dwarf runs behind the Rock Man and swings his warhammer against its back. The Rock Man groans in pain as the Dwarf lands another blow with his weapon. The third strike of the hammer has the desired effect and the Rock Man loosens its grip on you. Fragments of rock splinter off it as it slumps to the ground under a rain of hammer-blows. Satisfied that the Rock Man will not serve Evil again, you give the order to march on. Turn to **114**.

337

The night ashore passes without incident, but at first light you hear a loud buzzing noise. A swarm of large, black Harpoon Flies swoops down to attack your waking troops. Under the rain of poisoned, needle-like spikes, your men raise their shields to the sky. Roll one die. If you roll 1–3, turn to **69**. If you roll 4–6, turn to **83**.

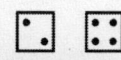

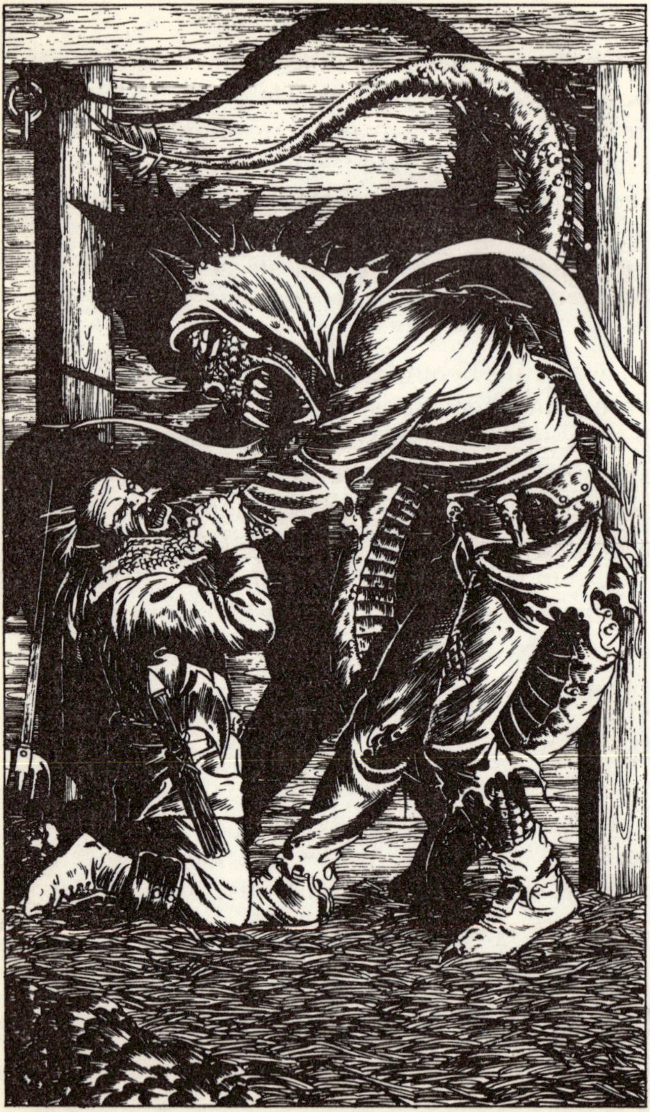

338

As you pass by an open stable door, you hear the sound of a scuffle coming from inside. You peer round the door and see a Dwarf on his knees trying to pull the clawed hands of his reptilian attacker away from his throat. His adversary is green and scaly and its spines have burst through its brown clothing. A long tail swishes from side to side and a forked tongue flicks in and out of its long-toothed jaw. 'Help!' cries the Dwarf. 'A Shapechanger has got me.' If you wish to help the Dwarf, turn to **22**. If you would rather walk on, turn to **149**.

339

At such short range the crossbow bolt is deadly. Its sharp tip pierces your neck and you fall down among the other brave soldiers who died to save Allansia. Demoralized by your death, your army turns and flees. Agglax is victorious.

340

Dead men don't make good warriors, and you curse your decision to waste your time and energy on a fruitless journey to Claw. Deduct 1 point from your LUCK. Wasting no more time, you leave Claw and return to your waiting army. You then march south until you find a narrow fording place on the river. Once safely across, you turn your army south-east in the direction of Zengis. Turn to **49**.

341

'Fortune smiles on you,' the voice says slowly. 'So tell me, who is the goddess whose statue forms part of my fountain?' Will you reply:

Liriel?	Turn to 32
Libra?	Turn to 250

342

Your march round the marsh takes you past a wooden hut. If you want to stop to take a look inside the hut, turn to 77. If you would rather keep on marching, turn to 211.

343

There is some writing on the paper, but it is in a language that you do not understand. If you are carrying the Hopper, turn to 125. If you are not carrying the Hopper, turn to 294.

344

You try to jump backwards but are struck in the shoulder by the arrow. Deduct 2 points from your STAMINA. The Wyvern is steered skywards again by the Goblin as your troops rush to your aid. As soon as your wound is bandaged, you give the order to march on; privately, you wonder if the attack from the air had been an assassination attempt on behalf of Agglax. Turn to **220**.

345

You have walked twenty yards down the tunnel when you are suddenly bowled over by a huge, hairy beast that leaps at you from out of the shadows. Pain burns down your back from gashes made by its powerful claws. Deduct 2 points from your STAMINA. Your torch is knocked to the floor but, miraculously, stays alight. Trapped in its underground cell, the Nandibear is berserk with rage and craves the taste of human flesh. You struggle to escape from its giant claws. Roll two dice. If the total is the same as or less than your SKILL score, turn to **66**. If the total is greater than your SKILL score, turn to **103**.

346

The barrel floats by; idly you wonder what it may have contained as it disappears from view. Turn to **209**.

347

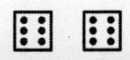

The girl slips the Gold Piece into her shirt pocket and leans over to whisper in your ear. 'The owner doesn't like winners at the best of times, but strangers winning is more than he can tolerate. I'd leave by the back door if I were you.' She seems to be speaking the truth, so you slip quietly out of the hall by the back door and, keeping in the shadows whenever possible, make your way back to the inn. Turn to **50**.

348

The man's head slowly turns towards you and in a slow, deep voice he asks, 'What kind of bet?' You point to two spilt blobs of jam on the table and tell him that he can choose one of them and you will have the other. Then you simply wait for one of the many flies in the tavern to land on either his jam or your jam. Whichever blob is landed on first gives victory. The man grunts and asks, 'What's the bet?' 'My 10 Gold Pieces against that gold brooch on your tunic,' you reply. 'Make it 50 Gold Pieces,' the man snaps back. If you wish to bet 50 Gold Pieces, turn to **161**. If you would rather abandon the idea of a bet and ask the man his name instead, turn to **3**.

349

You walk through a section of the forest where there are several mounds of earth into which clay dolls have been half buried. If you wish to take one of the dolls, turn to **226**. If you would rather leave them where they are and press on, turn to **134**.

350

Walking upriver along the bank, you pass six old oak trees. One of the trees has long since died but has a door set in its trunk. If you are curious enough to open the door, turn to **167**. If you would rather keep going towards Claw, turn to **399**.

351

Desperately outnumbered, you call the retreat and run back with your five Knights to your reserve troops. Your ears ring with the tormenting cries of the victorious Chaos Warriors. Expecting them to attack again, you scream out your battle orders. But the warriors turn and trot back to rejoin the rest of the evil army. You decide that attack is the best form of defence and give the order for your army to march towards the front line of Trolls. Turn to **178**.

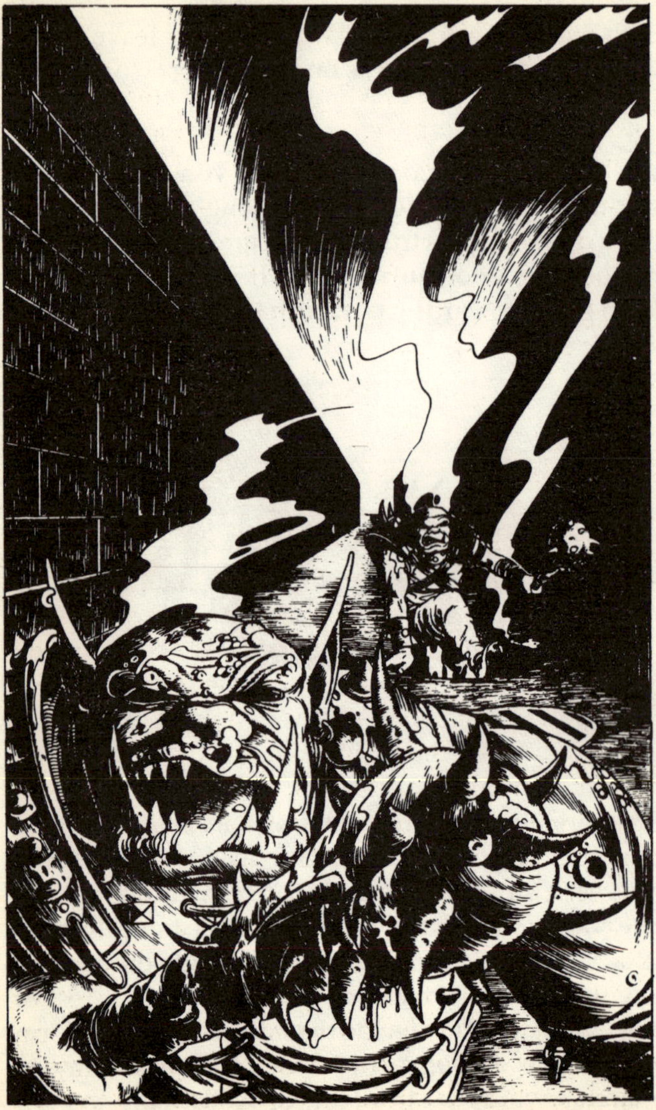

352

Walking down the alley, you tread on an iron grate. As you pass over it, the grate suddenly flies into the air and two ugly brown creatures scramble out of the tunnel beneath the grate. Covered in warts and dripping in sewage, two foul-smelling Sewer Goblins, armed with spiked clubs, run forward to ambush you. Fight them one at a time.

	SKILL	STAMINA
First SEWER GOBLIN	6	5
Second SEWER GOBLIN	6	5

If you win, turn to **251**.

353

Captain Barnock has the *Flying Toucan* moored to the riverbank long before the pirate ship is upon it, and you order your men to jump ashore. Quickly you line up the Elven Archers along the bank and order them to be ready to fire on the command. When the pirate ship is close enough, you shout across to its captain, telling him not to ram the *Flying Toucan* as there is no treasure on board. If he wants treasure, he will have to come ashore and fight for it. You see the pirate captain examining your troops through his telescope and you smile, satisfied that he will be surprised to encounter such a strong force. Your plan works; the pirate captain shouts out new orders to his men, and you watch the pirate ship sail past the *Flying Toucan*, downriver and out of sight. Add 1 point to your LUCK. Captain Barnock begins to cheer loudly, until a coughing fit overtakes

354–356

him and he has to sit down to recover. But in less than half an hour, all your troops and baggage are aboard the *Flying Toucan* once more, and you set sail upriver for Zengis. Turn to **175**.

354

You step warily into the mouth, expecting a stone slab to fall on top of you or a row of iron spikes to shoot out from the wall. But nothing happens and you are able to walk on. Turn to **53**.

355

Vine is a skilful wrestler and somehow manages to wriggle free from your grip. Before you realize what is happening, the roles are reversed and your arms are twisted behind your back in a painful hold. You try with all your might to break free but, the more you struggle, the more it hurts. In the end you have no choice but to submit. Turn to **213**.

356

Twenty of your valiant troops lie dead or dying on the battlefield. (Reduce the size of your army by this amount on the *Adventure Sheet*.) Trolls are trying to push the brave survivors back, while Goblins and Orcs are attacking the flanks remorselessly. Berserk with battle-lust, some of the Goblins and Orcs at the back fight among themselves, so eager are they to feel the clash of steel. To your right you see a Warrior being attacked from both sides by two Goblins. To your left, another Warrior is being clubbed to the ground by a Hill Troll. If you wish to help the Warrior on your left, turn to **269**. If you wish to help the Warrior on your right, turn to **62**.

357

The tavern is quite small inside and there are not many customers. The atmosphere seems friendly, so you make your way over to the bar to ask if the barman knows of any guides. He points to a table in the far corner and says, 'Ask old Thog over there. He used to be the best.' You walk over to the table and sit down next to an old battle-scarred warrior. You explain that you want to hire a guide. 'Where do you want to go?' he asks in a deep voice. Will you reply:

Through the Forest of Fiends?	Turn to **319**
To the Starstone Caves?	Turn to **57**

358

Laas reaches inside his furs and pulls out a long, curved tooth, attached to a leather thong. 'This is the tooth of a Yeti,' Laas says with pride. 'If you wear it, you will never be attacked by Werewolves or any other Lycanthropes. It is my wish that you should have it, as you are prepared to die to save Allansia.' You let Laas place the tooth round your neck and then tell him as much as you know about the Shadow Demon as you sail on upriver. Turn to **203**.

359

The Chaos Warriors are vicious fighters and they also outnumber your Knights by two to one. If your Knights include five White Knights, turn to **118**. If there are no White Knights in your army, turn to **317**.

360

With lightning speed, you dive to one side as the fireball crashes on to the ground where you were standing. You scramble to your feet just as the Goblin rider looses its arrow at you. Roll one die. If you roll 1, turn to **304**. If you roll between 2 and 4, turn to **344**. If you roll 5, turn to **147**. If you roll 6, turn to **283**.

361

You rush to the Dwarf's side and find that he is still breathing. 'Pills!' he gasps. 'Pills in my pouch . . . give me one . . . Hurry.' You do as he asks and give him one of the three green pills from his pouch. In less than a minute he has revived completely – even the wounds on his neck are beginning to heal. 'A wizard gave me the pills as reward for saving his life. Now I'm going to give you one of them for saving mine,' says the happy Dwarf. (You may use this pill at any time except during combat. It will restore 8 points of STAMINA.)

The Dwarf goes on to tell you how the Shape-changer had created an illusion to make itself appear as an old man; in this guise it entered the Dwarf's stable on the pretext of wishing to buy a donkey. 'As soon as we went inside, it attacked me and began to change back to its original form. Thanks to you I'm still alive. Look through its clothing and help yourself to any booty you find.' You reach down and rummage through the torn clothing. In an inside pocket you discover a gold seal with the number '332' stamped on it. 'Not bad,' exclaims the Dwarf as you spin the seal up in the air and catch it with your other hand. You say farewell to the Dwarf and go back into the street. Turn to **149**.

362

You walk further along the tunnel of the Nandi-bear's lair, wondering who locked the beast under the ground in the first place. And why? At the end of the tunnel you find nothing but a pile of old bone-covered straw. Unable to solve the mystery, you leave the lair and walk out of the clearing. Turn to **315**.

363

The guards are wearing chainmail and helmets and are each armed with a spear and a shield. Fight them one at a time.

	SKILL	STAMINA
First TOWN GUARD	8	7
Second TOWN GUARD	8	8

If you win, turn to **78**.

364

You wait anxiously for an hour, but thankfully do not develop a fever. You have escaped catching the terrible affliction of lycanthropy. The rest of the night passes without incident and in the morning you lead your army out of the forest, across the new plain. Turn to **323**.

365

The dagger strikes the hilt of your sword which is tucked in your belt and falls harmlessly to the ground. You suddenly realize that it would have been foolish to have taken the statue if the Wood Elves' attackers had left it alone. But you are alive and the statue is yours. Finding nothing else of interest, you decide to return to your army. Turn to **88**.

366

The rest of the day passes without incident and, as the light begins to fade, you give the order to set up camp. The mood of your men is very sombre and hardly a word is spoken round the campfire. After the guards are posted, nobody wastes any time in lying down to sleep. Turn to **279**.

367

Half an hour after eating the apples, some of the soldiers become ill, yourself included. Deduct 3 points from your STAMINA and 1 point from your SKILL. Their health quickly deteriorates, and two die quite quickly. Before the day is over, ten have died in total: make the deduction on your *Adventure Sheet* and also deduct 1 point from your LUCK. You regret your decision to give the apples to your men, and resolve not to be distracted from your main objective in future. Turn to **209**.

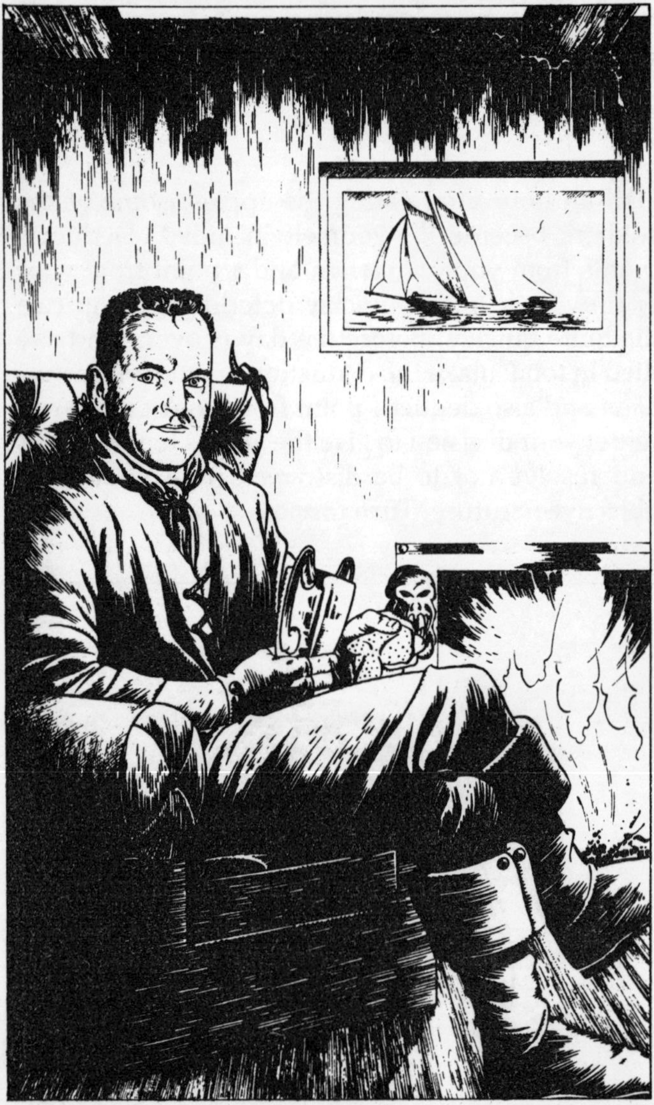

368

The door opens into a small reception room which has low oak beams and white walls. In the wall opposite, a fire is burning in the hearth, and above it is a painting of a small sailing boat. A man is sitting in a high-backed leather chair in front of the fire, vigorously polishing a silver cup. You clear your throat to get his attention and he turns towards you and says, 'I beg your pardon, but I didn't hear you come in. As you can see, I'm busy polishing up this cup we won at sailing. But I don't want to bore you with my sailing stories. A room will cost you 2 Gold Pieces, including breakfast.' You pay for the room and wait for the man to give you the key. He stands up, but instead leans against the hearth and looks admiringly at the painting. 'Ah, *Harem* was a great boat with a great crew. We left all the other boats clean behind and won all our races except for one, and that was lost only because of Spike's navigation.' If you want to butt in and ask the man for the key, turn to **81**. If you are prepared to be patient and listen to the man's story, turn to **183**.

369

'Might I suggest that you buy this wonderful little Hopper,' the old man says with a smile, pointing to the kangaroo-like creature that you were watching a few moments ago. 'His name is Roob and he'll perch on your shoulder quite happily all day long – although he can hop along at walking pace if you tire of him sitting on you. Not only does Roob speak, he can also cast an invisibility spell on himself, and on you too, if he happens to be sitting on your shoulder. Just say "One, one, one," and *puff*, you're invisible. He also understands the Troll tongue. All I'm asking for Roob is 50 Gold Pieces.' If you wish to buy the Hopper, turn to **335**. If you would rather leave the shop without buying the familiar, turn to **218**.

370

You drag the Blog out of the tree and bind its arms behind its back with a length of vine. You begin to ask it questions about its village and about Agglax, but the Blog understands only a few words of the human tongue and is unable to reply. Will you:

Kill the Blog?	Turn to **29**
Gesture that you want treasure?	Turn to **247**
Set the Blog free?	Turn to **169**

371

The axe whistles past your head and clatters on the street in front of you. You stop for a moment to pick it up and then run off again, leaving the lumbering Axeman behind. Turn to **52**.

372

You walk along the tunnel for a few yards – but in the gloom you do not see a tripwire which is stretched across the floor. You catch your foot in it, causing a massive slab of ceiling rock to crash down on top of you. You are killed instantly.

373

You just manage to grab hold of Vine's left ankle as he tries to leap over you, and you pull him to the ground. You scramble on top of him and try to pin him down with an arm-lock. Roll two dice. If the total is the same as or less than your SKILL score, turn to **237**. If the total is greater than your SKILL score, turn to **355**.

374

The Werewolf's long jaw bites down on the neck of the guard. It then turns to face you, its fangs dripping with blood. You must fight the Werewolf.

WEREWOLF   SKILL 8   STAMINA 9

If you win the fight without losing one Attack Round, turn to **305**. If you lost one or more Attack Rounds and yet still killed the Werewolf, turn to **228**.

375

By now many of your men are awake, although five Warriors are found who will never wake again. Their throats have been cut by the midnight raider and the gold rings cut from their fingers. If only you had awoken earlier, this might never have happened. The lookout is found nursing a sore head, having been attacked from behind; an extra man is put on watch for the rest of the night. Not long after dawn, Captain Barnock gives the order to set sail upriver. Turn to **188**.

376

You lock the door behind you and slump gratefully into the soft bed. You are asleep in seconds and do not wake until the morning, when there is a loud knocking at the door. 'Breakfast is ready!' shouts Obigee. After a large plate of ham and eggs you feel ready to take on Agglax himself. The peaceful sleep and plentiful food have done you a lot of good. Add 2 points to your STAMINA. You finally say farewell to Obigee and walk out into the street. After walking less than a hundred yards, the street ends at a junction. If you wish to go left, turn to **65**. If you wish to turn right, turn to **268**.

377

You walk into the tunnel and soon arrive at a junction. If you wish to go left, turn to **85**. If you wish to go right, turn to **214**.

378

You sit down at the table and greet the man sitting there; he is dressed in dark-brown leather armour over black robes. But the man remains silent, the vacant expression on his face unchanged. His staring eyes remain fixed on the door as he raises his mug to his lips and gulps down his ale. Will you:

Ask him his name?	Turn to **3**
Move to the table with the vagabonds?	Turn to **18**
Challenge him to a bet?	Turn to **348**

379

No sooner have you drawn your sword from your adversary's body than another moves forward to take its place. If you wish to continue fighting, turn to **193**. If you would rather try to distract the enemy by throwing all your gold into the air, turn to **394**.

380

The Elves line up along the side of the ship and fire their arrows at the surprised Raiders. Their aim is deadly: eight Raiders are killed with the first volley. The remaining Raiders realize it would be suicidal to press home their attack, and turn their canoes around to paddle back to shore as quickly as possible. A great cheer goes up from the deck of the ship as you sail upriver, away from the routed Raiders. Turn to **309**.

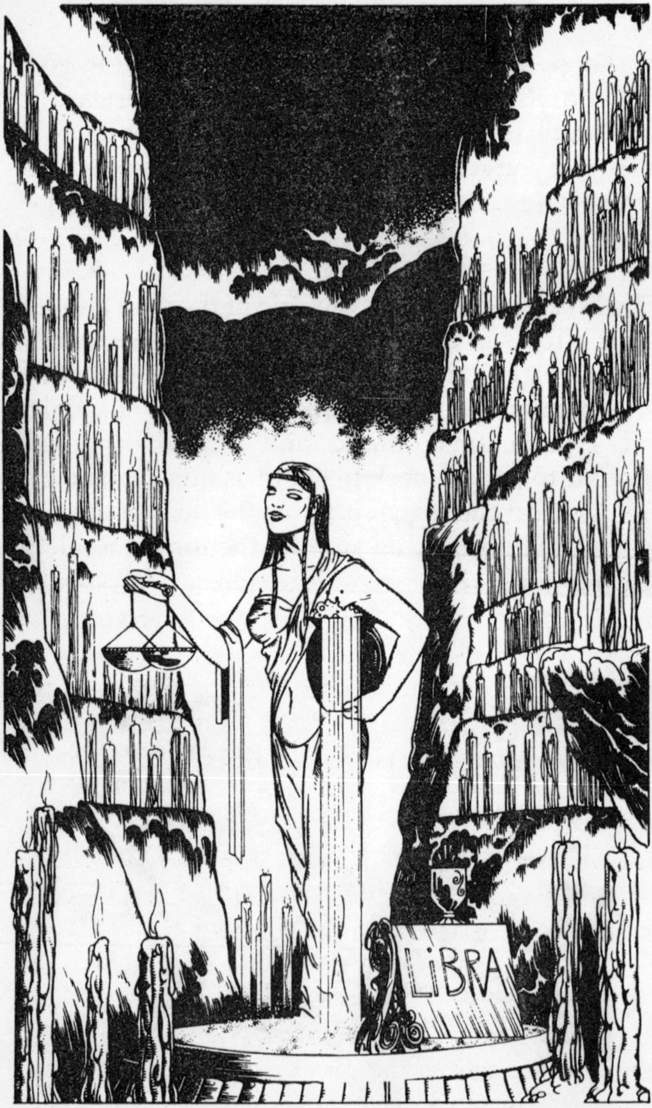
LiBRA

381

The passageway opens out into a high-ceilinged cave, brightly lit by hundreds of burning candles. In the middle is a marble fountain carved in the shape of a young goddess, dressed in long robes. Water trickles from an urn which she is holding under her left arm and in her right hand she holds a pair of scales; a metal cup rests on top of a plaque in which the word 'Libra' is etched. If you wish to drink some water from the fountain, turn to **11**. If you would rather walk through the cave and down the passage in the wall opposite, turn to **221**.

382

After passing a row of old wooden houses you come across a curious shop. There is nothing displayed in the window except straw and an empty birdcage. Brown paint is flaking off the window-frame and also the door, above which is a sign which reads: 'Pets – normal and unnatural'. If you want to enter the pet shop, turn to **112**. If you would rather keep on walking, turn to **218**.

383

The crossbow bolt lodges in your throat with a sickening thud. You fall to the floor, clutching your throat, and are dead within minutes.

384

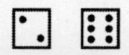

A rope securing a block and tackle in the rigging above you parts as the pirate ship rams the *Flying Toucan*. The block and tackle crash to the deck, narrowly missing you. You run to look over the side of the ship and see a gaping hole through which water is pouring in. There is no time to lose as the *Flying Toucan* starts to sink; you order your men to abandon ship and swim to the north bank. There is much shouting and panic coming from Captain Barnock's crew as you dive into the cold river. The water is not very deep; looking back you see the pirates boarding the half-submerged old ship. A few minutes later, you haul yourself out of the water and count the cost of the sinking of the *Flying Toucan*. Roll one die. If you roll 1–3, turn to **7**. If you roll 4–6, turn to **313**.

385

You congratulate Max on her excellent swordsmanship as she shakes your hand. You tell her to meet Lexon at your camp outside Zengis where she will receive her payment of 300 Gold Pieces (deduct this from your *Adventure Sheet*). 'You will not regret hiring us,' she says as she leads her men away. You watch her for a few moments, before turning the corner of the street. Turn to **314**.

386

Your army fights a *Skirmish Battle* against the fifty Fire Imps. If you win, turn to **316**.

387

As you step on one of the floorboards, it tilts forward and the cotton holding the sword slips off the spike. The sword drops straight down on to the Elf but, to your surprise, merely bounces off her stomach. 'Untie me,' she begs, 'and I will explain!' If you wish to untie her, turn to **243**. If you would rather leave this strange Elf and return to your men outside, turn to **320**.

388

The crowd goes wild as Big Belly Man celebrates victory once again. In his now familiar way, he punches the air with his hands and roars in satisfaction. You waste no time in making your way to the exit, feeling more than a little sick after gorging yourself on the foul pie. Deduct 1 point from your STAMINA. Feeling rather like an inflated Bloodbeast, you walk off along the street. Turn to **95**.

389

You keep a watchful eye on the clearing as you walk round it to rejoin the narrow path through the undergrowth. *Test your Luck*. If you are Lucky, turn to **162**. If you are Unlucky, turn to **308**.

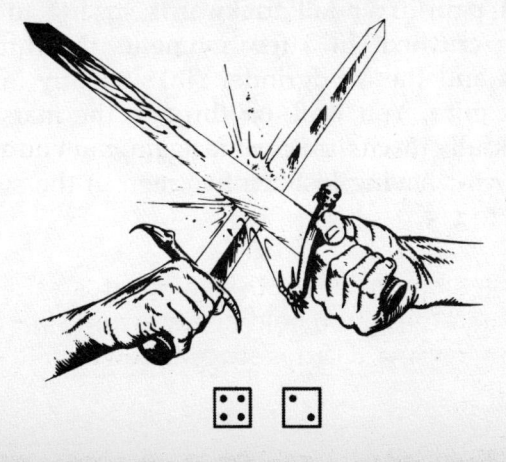

390

Laas looks aggrieved and walks off to join his men. A few minutes later he returns and says, 'Here are your 100 Gold Pieces. We shall not be coming with you, since we are deeply insulted.' You cannot change the Northmen's minds and have to let them disembark. Deduct 1 point from your LUCK. Feeling slightly dispirited, you give the order to sail on upriver. Turn to **203**.

391

'You are wrong,' the Knight says sharply. 'Go back whence you came.' If you wish to turn your army round and march south along the edge of the chasm, turn to **327**. If you would rather attack the Knights, turn to **148**.

392

The point of your sword finds its mark, sinking into the soft yellow flesh. Thick green fluid pours from the wound as the Mudgrinder thrashes around in blind pain. You fall backwards, trying to avoid being crushed. In a few moments the thrashing stops and the Mudgrinder sinks silently into the black mire. You walk on through the marsh and thankfully reach firm ground again, but you are still angry for having lost the five men in the swamp. Turn to **115**.

393

The tunnel grows noticeably warmer and is now also bathed in a soft, purple light. As you walk on, it gets even hotter and the light becomes brighter. You begin to sweat and have to squint to reduce the glare of the strong purple light. Suddenly the floor gives way beneath you, and you find yourself sliding, feet first, down a steep, coiling chute. You see the end of the chute coming but are sliding too quickly to be able to stop yourself from falling out. You land with a splash in a pool of hot purple liquid, which is situated in the centre of another cave. You climb out of the pool and realize that purple light envelops you, radiating out from your body. If you drank the water from the fountain earlier, turn to **42**. If you did not drink there, turn to **160**.

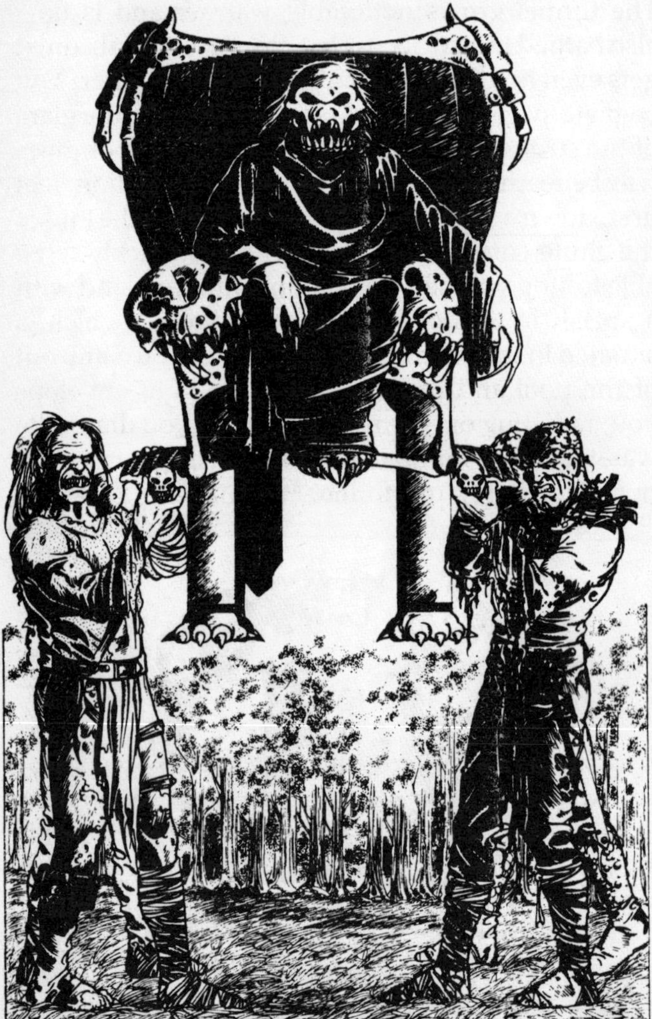

394

The Gold Pieces fall through the air like huge golden droplets of rain. Confusion immediately takes hold of the enemy, as the Trolls and Goblins scramble to pick up the gold they so love. Oblivious to the main battle, they fight one another ferociously to claim the fallen treasure. You seize your opportunity and break through the disorganized ranks. Suddenly you see the Demon you have been hunting. Sitting calmly in a sedan chair supported by four hideous Zombies, Agglax watches you approach through blood-red eyes. He makes no move as you get nearer. Only his vile head and taloned hands show from his black robes, a sight which sends a terrible shiver down your back. Sensing danger at Agglax's calmness, you wonder how you should attack him. Will you:

Use a pendant (if you have one)?	Turn to 236
Use a crystal (if you have one)?	Turn to 39
Use your sword?	Turn to 301

395

The vagabonds' interest increases when you mention that you are willing to pay for information about Agglax. 'We know where this Agglax is building his army and we can mark the place on a map,' says Laz, sensing the smell of gold. 'But,' he continues with a smug grin on his face, 'more importantly, we know how to help you defeat the Shadow Demon. For 10 Gold Pieces, we'll show you where Agglax is. For another 90 Gold Pieces, we'll tell you how to weaken him.' If you want to pay the vagabonds 10 Gold Pieces, turn to **322**. If you are willing to pay 100 Gold Pieces, turn to **56**.

396

You fall back against the trunk and quickly regain your balance. The Blog blows another dart down at you, but it bounces harmlessly off your shield. You seize the opportunity, climb quickly upwards and grab hold of the Blog's ankle before it can reload its blowpipe. You tug on it hard and the Blog drops its blowpipe trying to hang on to the branch. But after a brief struggle it gives up and slumps back against the trunk, its head bowed, to await the punishment of your sword. If you wish to kill the Blog, turn to **82**. If you would rather interrogate it, turn to **370**.

397

You let out an agonized cry and clutch at your throat where the trident's spike is lodged. You fall forward and crash to the deck, slain by a lone Fish Man. Your adventure is over.

398

You lift the lid of the box and see nothing but brilliant white light inside. Pain fills your eyes and they feel as if they are burning. You blink several times but still can see nothing but white light. You have lost your vision to the Blinding Stone. Deduct 6 points from your SKILL and 2 points from your LUCK. You stumble back to your troops and call on Lexon to act as your eyes and guide. Despite this tragedy, you are determined to go on and shout out the order to march. Turn to **181**.

399

About an hour later, a voice behind you suddenly shouts, 'Look! Look up to the skies in the east. A flying creature with a rider.' You look up to see a lizard-like creature with great green leathery wings swooping down towards you – it's a Wyvern, and its Goblin rider is aiming its bow straight at you. The Wyvern's mouth roars open to send a bursting ball of flame down at you. Roll one die. If you roll a 1, turn to **97**. If you roll between 2 and 5, turn to **207**. If you roll a 6, turn to **360**.

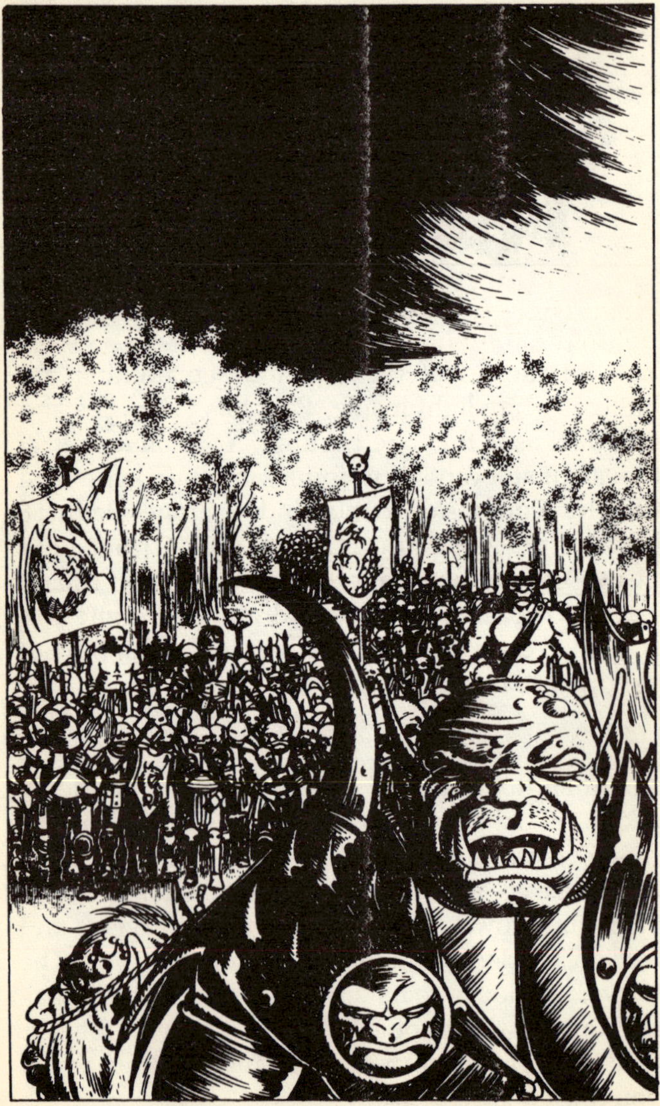

400

On witnessing Agglax's destruction, the creatures of the Army of Death go berserk. The various tribes attack one another, each blaming the others for the loss of their leader. You try to get them to surrender, but they are hell-bent on self-destruction. In the end you leave the Goblins, Orcs, Hill Trolls, Zombies and Elite Fanatics to encompass their own annihilation, while you march your army back to Fang in triumph. But how long will it be before a new peril threatens your beloved Allansia?

The Official Fighting Fantasy website

www.fightingfantasygamebooks.com

Visit the Fighting Fantasy website for ...

- The Adventurers' Guild, the Official Fighting Fantasy Club!
- Latest news on FF Gamebooks and events
- Exclusive interviews with Steve Jackson and Ian Livingstone
- Competitions and games
- Monster gallery
- Advance information on all forthcoming Gamebooks, including previews of cover art
- Download screensavers, wallpaper, masks, doorhangers, bookmarks, and much more ...

JOIN THE ADVENTURERS' GUILD
THE OFFICIAL FF CLUB

FREE MEMBERSHIP

Sign up for the Adventurers' Guild, the Official Fighting Fantasy Club, at *www.fightingfantasygamebooks.com!*

As a member, you will receive FREE OF CHARGE ...

- A **monthly newsletter** packed with all the latest on Gamebooks and events, opportunities to receive exclusive goodies and posters, info on forthcoming books, Club competitions, and much more ...

- An **'Adventurers' Pack'**, including Adventure Sheet, two Gaming Dice, a photocard of Steve Jackson and Ian Livingstone, creators of Fighting Fantasy, an exclusive piece of artwork from an FF cover, and a Membership Card valid for two years.

- An **FF card** on your birthday

Members can also use their password to gain access to the **Members' Space** on the FF website, where you can post your views to other members on the Message Forum, chat to other members online and gain access to exclusive material weeks before it's released onto the main site.

™

Join the ADVENTURERS' GUILD today at

www.fightingfantasygamebooks.com!

The Warlock of Firetop Mountain
Steve Jackson and Ian Livingstone

Deep in the caverns beneath Firetop Mountain lies an untold wealth of treasure, guarded by a powerful Warlock – or so the rumour goes. Several adventurers like yourself have set off for Firetop Mountain in search of the Warlock's hoard. None has ever returned. Do you dare follow them?

Your quest is to find the Warlock's treasure, hidden deep within a dungeon populated with a multitude of terrifying monsters. You will need courage, determination and a fair amount of luck if you are to survive all the traps and battles, and reach your goal – the innermost chambers of the Warlock's domain.

UK £4.99 • Canada $9.99 • ISBN 1 84046 387 2

The Citadel of Chaos
Steve Jackson

Deep inside the Citadel of Chaos, the dread sorcerer Balthus Dire is plotting the downfall of the goodfolk of the Vale of Willow. His battle plans are laid, his awesome army equipped, and attack is surely imminent.

Summoned by a desperate plea for help, YOU are the Vale of Willow's only hope. As star pupil of the Grand Wizard of Yore and a master sorcerer yourself, you must strike at the very heart of Balthus Dire's nightmare world. Though you command many powerful spells, the quest may be deadly, for who knows what creatures lie in wait in the Citadel of Chaos?

UK £4.99 • Canada $9.99 • ISBN 1 84046 389 9

Deathtrap Dungeon
Ian Livingstone

Down in the dark twisting labyrinth of Fang, unknown horrors await you. Devised by the devilish mind of Baron Sukumvit, the labyrinth is riddled with fiendish traps and bloodthirsty monsters, which will test your skills almost beyond the limit of endurance.

Countless adventurers before you have taken up the challenge of the Trial of Champions and walked through the carved mouth of the labyrinth, never to be seen again. Should you come out of the labyrinth alive, you will be wealthy beyond your dreams. Do YOU dare enter?

UK £4.99 • Canada $9.99 • ISBN 1 84046 388 0

Creature of Havoc
Steve Jackson

Evil is festering in Trolltooth Pass. The necromancer Zharradan Marr is close to stealing the secrets of Elven magic which would make him invincible. Nothing could then prevent his legions of Chaos from taking over the whole of Allansia …

But what do you know or care about all this? In this unique adventure, YOU are the Creature of Havoc, a monstrous beast with a taste for fighting. Ruled only by hunger and rage, you have no knowledge of your past or destiny. If you survive, you may begin to control your bestial nature and learn your true purpose, but success is by no means certain, for the traps and terrors of Trolltooth Pass are many …

UK £4.99 • Canada $9.99 • ISBN 1 84046 391 0

City of Thieves
Ian Livingstone

Terror stalks the night as Zanbar Bone and his bloodthirsty Moon Dogs hold the prosperous town of Silverton to ransom. YOU are an adventurer, a sword for hire, and the merchants of Silverton turn to you in their hour of need.

Your mission takes you along the dark, twisting streets of Port Blacksand to seek the help of the wizard Nicodemus. But Blacksand is riddled with thieves, assassins and foul creatures. Should you survive, you must journey to the most terrible place of all – the tower stronghold of the Night Prince himself, Zanbar Bone!

UK £4.99 • Canada $9.99 • ISBN 1 84046 397 X

Crypt of the Sorcerer
Ian Livingstone

An ancient evil is stirring in the bowels of the earth, and the land is blighted. After being entombed for one hundred years, the necromancer Razaak has been re-awoken and is poised to fulfil his promise of death and tyranny. His army of undead are at large across Allansia bringing death and destruction to all who resist.

It is up to YOU to find the only weapon to which Razaak is vulnerable – his own magic sword! Only then might you survive the dangers that await you in his evil lair – the Crypt of the Sorcerer!

UK £4.99 • Canada $9.99 • ISBN 1 84046 396 1

House of Hell
Steve Jackson

Stranded miles from anywhere on a dark and stormy night, your only hope of refuge is the strange, ramshackle mansion you can see in the distance ...

But entering the House of Hell hurls you into an adventure of spine-chilling and blood-curdling terror. The dangers of the torrential storm outside are nothing compared to the nightmarish creatures that await you within its gruesome walls.

Be warned! You must try to keep your fear under control – collect too many FEAR points and you will die of fright. Can you make it through the night without being scared – to *death*?

UK £4.99 • Canada $9.99 • ISBN 1 84046 417 8

The Forest of Doom
Ian Livingstone

Only the mad or the very brave would willingly risk a journey into Darkwood Forest. Yet it is here you must go to find the missing pieces of the legendary Hammer of Stonebridge. Fashioned by the Dwarfs many ages ago, only the war-hammer can protect peaceful Stonebridge against its ancient doom.

Warned of the monstrous creatures that lurk in Darkwood's tangled forest, you must first find Yaztromo, the master mage, whose magic may help protect you. But time is short. Can you restore the Hammer before the Trolls destroy Stonebridge for ever?

UK £4.99 • Canada $9.99 • ISBN 1 84046 429 1

Caverns of the Snow Witch
Ian Livingstone

On the trail of a hideous creature that is terrorising the northern trade routes, you find its last victim – still alive, but barely. With his dying breath he lays a great burden on your shoulders ...

After years of searching he has found the entrance to the Crystal Caves of the evil Snow Witch, high up in the Icefinger Mountains. She must be destroyed before her dark powers bring on another ice age and Allansia slips under her dominion for ever. But time is running out. Can you slay the vile Snow Witch before she becomes all powerful?

UK £4.99 • Canada $9.99 • ISBN 1 84046 432 1

Trial of Champions
Ian Livingstone

At last – a return to Deathtrap Dungeon!

Since the day your boat was rammed by pirates, you have been galley-slave aboard their ship. When at last you reach land, things go from bad to worse. For this is Blood Island and you must serve as unwilling slave to Lord Carnuss – the evil brother of Baron Sukumvit, who created Deathtrap Dungeon!

Should you survive the gladiatorial games of Lord Carnuss, you will enter the Dungeon. But the twisted mind of Baron Sukumvit has completely redesigned the deadly labyrinth of Fang. New traps and terrors, mazes and monsters, await you at every turn. Can you survive this Trial of Champions and free yourself from slavery?

UK £4.99 • Canada $9.99 • ISBN 1 84046 434 8

Return to Firetop Mountain
Ian Livingstone

Firetop Mountain, the forbidding peak whose dark shadow once cast gloom over the whole of Northern Allansia, has been quiet for ten years. It has been that long since the diabolical reign of the evil sorcerer, Zagor, was brought to an end.

But now, resurrected by the power of dark sorcery, Zagor has risen from the dead! More evil than before, the crazed wizard is intent only on wreaking his revenge upon all in Allansia. He must be stopped, and for good this time. Some brave adventurer – YOU! – must enter the forbidding labyrinth and bring justice once more to the lord of Firetop Mountain!

UK £4.99 • Canada $9.99 • ISBN 1 84046 481 X
Published December 2003

Island of the Lizard King
Ian Livingstone

Kidnapped by a vicious race of Lizard Men from Fire Island, the young men of Oyster Bay face a grim future of slavery, starvation and a lingering death. Their new master is the mad and dangerous Lizard King, who holds sway over his land of mutants by the eerie powers of black magic and voodoo. YOU are the only one who can hope to rescue the suffering prisoners, but do you have the courage to risk this dangerous mission?

UK £4.99 • Canada $9.99 • ISBN 1 84046 491 7
Published December 2003

Sorcery! 1: The Shamutanti Hills
Steve Jackson

Based on the best-selling *Fighting Fantasy* Gamebook system, *The Shamutanti Hills* is Book One in Steve Jackson's *Sorcery!* series. Your epic quest will take you across the mysterious hills to the cityport of Kharé, but only if you outwit the creatures, traps and wizardry you encounter along the way.

Play as either a warrior or as a wizard. If you choose wizardry, your survival will depend on your knowledge of the *Sorcery!* Spell Book's darkest secrets. With many other unique features to discover, *Sorcery!* is a true challenge for novice and veteran adventurers alike.

UK £5.99 • Canada $9.99 • ISBN 1 84046 430 5

Sorcery! 2: Kharé – Cityport of Traps
Steve Jackson

Kharé, where every doorway and alley may conceal sudden danger – or unexpected help!

As a warrior relying on force of arms, or a wizard trained in magic, you must brave the terror of a city built to trap the unwary. You will need all your wits about you to survive the unimaginable horrors ahead and to make sense of the clues which may lead to your success – or to your doom!

Based on the best-selling *Fighting Fantasy* gamebook system, *Kharé: Cityport of Traps* is Book Two in Steve Jackson's *Sorcery!* series.

UK £5.99 • Canada $9.99 • ISBN 1 84046 433 X

Sorcery! 3: The Seven Serpents
Steve Jackson

Your quest to recover the Crown of Kings has led you to the brutal wilderness of the Baklands, on the far side of which lies the dark Mampang Fortress. Seven serpents with elemental powers speed ahead of you, intent on warning the evil Archmage of Mampang of your coming. Can you slay all seven before they reach him?

The Seven Serpents is Book Three of Steve Jackson's four-part *Sorcery!* epic, based on the best-selling *Fighting Fantasy* gamebook system. Play as either a sword-wielding warrior or a spell-casting wizard. Each *Sorcery!* book is a complete adventure – you don't need to have read a previous book to move on to the next.

UK £5.99 • Canada $9.99 • ISBN 1 84046 435 6

Sorcery! 4: The Crown of Kings
Steve Jackson

The Crown of Kings is the final part of Steve Jackson's *Sorcery!* epic. The legendary Crown of Kings is at last within your grasp – or is it?

At the end of your long trek, you face the unknown terrors of the Mampang Fortress. Somewhere within these walls the dreaded Archmage is hidden and, with him, the legendary Crown of Kings you have risked so much for. But beware! For if you have not defeated the Seven Serpents, your arrival has been anticipated …

UK £5.99 • Canada $9.99 • ISBN 1 84046 438 0
Published September 2003

Also from Wizard Books

Joshua Cross
Diane Redmond

It is only when a monstrous centaur appears from nowhere to chase him along the Thames Embankment that Joshua Cross becomes aware of his destiny.

Swept back in time to Ancient Greece, Josh begins an epic journey that will lead him to the very depths of the Underworld. But before he can return home, Josh must face the man who destroyed his father and who wants to kill *him* alone.

UK £4.99 • Canada $12.00 • ISBN 1 84046 466 6

Joshua Cross and the Queen's Conjuror
Diane Redmond

Joshua Cross's enemy, Leirtod, is back with a vengeance ...

Swept back to 1590s London and placed in the care of Dr Dee, the Queen's Conjuror – a mathematician, astrologer, and occasional dabbler in the occult – Joshua soon discovers that his friend Dido is in mortal danger.

With Dee's aid Josh must reach her before Leirtod does and death is dealt. Dee, however, is surrounded by his own demons: spies set up to burn him for his Catholic sympathies.

This is an action-packed novel that treads the dark side of the Elizabethan court where treachery and intrigue abound.

UK £10.00 • Canada $20.00 • ISBN 1 84046 487 9
Published October 2003

The Master of the Rings
Inside the World of J.R.R. Tolkien
Susan Ang

J.R.R. Tolkien is the greatest fantasy writer ever to have lived. He has millions of devoted readers worldwide, and now has a new legion of fans, thanks to the film versions of *The Lord of the Rings*.

The Master of the Rings takes a look at the man himself, where he came from, what influenced his writing, and the themes that unite his major works. There's also a detailed guide to who's who, what's what and where's where in Middle-earth, and a unique look at the historical background to *The Lord of the Rings*. This is the perfect companion to Tolkien's stories.

UK £5.99 • Canada $12.00 • USA $13.95 • ISBN 1 84046 423 2

Darkness Visible
Inside the World of Philip Pullman
Nicholas Tucker

Philip Pullman, best known for the award-winning *His Dark Materials* trilogy, is one of Britain's most challenging and original authors.

Darkness Visible looks at the strange world of *His Dark Materials* and its creator, discussing the sources that have influenced Pullman's many books, the themes throughout, and the controversy and criticism that Pullman has attracted. There's also a who's who of *His Dark Materials* as well as an answer to the exasperating question, 'What exactly is "dust"?' This is a fantastic guide to have to hand when reading any of Pullman's stories.

UK £5.99 • Canada $12.00 • ISBN 1 84046 482 8
Published November 2003

Big Numbers
A mind-expanding trip to infinity and back
Mary and John Gribbin
Illustrated by Ralph Edney and Nicholas Halliday

How big is infinity? How small is an electron?
When will the Sun destroy the Earth?
How fast is a nerve impulse in your brain?
Why can't you see inside a black hole?

Welcome to the amazing world of 'Big Numbers', where you'll travel from the furthest reaches of the known Universe to the tiniest particles that make up life on Earth. Together with Mary and John Gribbin, you can find out how our telescopes can see 10 billion years into the past, and why a thimble-full of a neutron star would contain as much mass as all the people on Earth put together!

Wizard Books UK £6.99 • Canada $15.00 • ISBN 1 84046 431 3